Where are we going?

Short stories for girls

S. Martin Drake

Copyright 2017 by Sandee Martin Drake

Create Space Publishing

2

All rights reserved. No part of this book may be used or reproduced by any means, electronic, graphic or mechanical, including photo copying, recording taping or by any information storage retrieval system without written permission of the author except in case of brief quotations embodied in critical articles and reviews.

This is a work of fictions. All characters, incidents, names or organizations and dialogue in this novel are either products of the author's imagination or are used fictitiously.

You may contact me at sandeedrake1@gmail.com

Front and back cover designed by J. A. Drake, graphic designer.
jadepr33@yahoo.com

In the chapters with French vocabulary, an English translation has the words surrounded by ( ) after the French word.

CHAPTER ONE

AN ADVENTURE BEGINS

1957, Prattville, Alabama

Today is THE DAY. I sat up suddenly in my bed. No, this isn't Christmas morning or my birthday, and the alarm hadn't awakened me. Something special was going to happen today. I snuggled down under my lightweight pink blanket and knew my life would change today after my brother, sister, and I came home from Prattville Elementary School.

"Mom, are you up?" I called out through the open door to the room just across the small hallway of our three bedroom rented house.

"Yes. Go back to sleep now, Sandra; you don't have to leave for another hour and a half. I told you last night, we won't know where we are going to move until after your dad lands his airplane."

"I remember, but I'm trying to guess which country . . . are you sure this is an overseas assignment?"

"Yes. Please go back to sleep or you'll be too tired to get through your busy day at school."

Later, in my sixth grade class, the hours seemed to drag on forever. Several of my friends came up to ask me if I heard where my family would be moving. Even my teacher, Miss Hazel Wilson, asked questions. She reminded me I would have a few extra days for the geography report. Miss Hazel had stated: "Writing about the new country your family will move to might help you adjust a little better by finding out helpful information. Then maybe you won't be so worried."

When the final bell rang, my younger sister Carole Anne, my younger brother Harvey and I were the first ones to race out for our bus. On the ride home, we mentioned a country we had picked and decided to give each other help for one chore on Saturday for whoever picked the right place.

"We're home, what's the place?" Carole Anne called out as she entered the living room first.

My mom sat on the sofa with baby Jon, giving him a bottle of milk, as she listened to some accordion music on the radio. She smiled at us, pleased with the enthusiasm we had been expressing over the last three months. My dad told her our next move would definitely be overseas.

"*Bonjour, mes enfants,*" she said carefully.

"What are you saying, Mom?" my brother asked, scrunching his dark brown eyebrows. "What language is this? Hey, you must already know; but, I don't see our car in the driveway. Where's Dad?"

"He isn't home yet, Harvey, but he called and told me the country. Who can guess what *Bonjour* means? Does the music I'm listening to give you a hint?" My mom smiled at our enthusiasm.

As the oldest at age 11, I answered right away. "I know the music is supposed to remind us of a specific country, right, Mom?" I looked at my younger sister and brother and grinned. "I am going to vote for France."

My six year old sister, Carole Anne looked surprised as she said, "I voted for the Hawaiian Islands." She pushed her long blond bangs off her forehead and frowned. My ten year old brother Harvey answered with "I was kinda hoping for Germany."

My mom looked pleased as she motioned for us to sit down on the couch. Then, she said, "Who wants to see what's on page forty-six?" She opened our Atlas book. This page showed a map of France.

"Yes, you are right, Sandra. We are going to France for the next three years. The words I said to you in French were hello my children. I called one of my friends who moved here from S.H.A.P.E. (Supreme Headquarters Allied Powers Europe) in Fontainebleau, France where we'll be going. She told me how to say this phrase."

All three of us started speaking at once, with one question after another.

"Now calm down for a minute. First of all, just for today, let's get the time frame settled so you can plan for this move. We will have time for all your questions as we figure out what has to be done. The Air Force will send someone over to look at our furniture next week. We will have a specific weight allowance to move our things and we will probably need to store some of our furniture until we get back."

"What is this time frame, Mom?" I asked. "Do we get to finish the school year or have to go right away?"

"Yeah, just for once I'd sure like to be able to finish a whole year in one school," Harvey said, scratching his dark brown hair.

"We'll be leaving one week after school is finished. First, we must get our passport pictures taken and then make sure all our shots are current. Next, we will drive up to New York and stay with my sister and her family, on Long Island." She put Jon in the playpen and smiled at us. "We'd like to take you around the city and have a few days to relax before we leave. We will be on board a military ship for ten days and each of us can only take two suitcases."

Carole Anne looked a little worried with creases on her freckled forehead. "Shots? What do you mean, Mommy? I thought we did all that stuff before we started school. I don't want any more."

"You're probably alright Carole Anne; however, we must be sure there aren't any new diseases in Europe."

"How long will this trip take? You know how we hate driving 'cause we never get to stop when dad drives us on a long trip." Harvey tapped his fingers on the coffee table, remembering some of our family vacations.

"Children, this is going to be one of the best moves our family has ever experienced. All the assignments we've taken have been in the northeast, except for one to Cape Canaveral in Florida. We will be going to a place where many customs are different from ours. They speak French, not English. In the three months we have left, I'm going to sign up for classes on base so I can, at least, have some idea of basic phrases."

When Major Miller arrived home an hour later we had settled down to the idea of crossing the Atlantic Ocean and living in a foreign country. At least this time, he would be here for the move instead of leaving my mom to handle all the details. Even though this wasn't his first overseas assignment, he recalled briefly how he hated his year in

Korea, alone. He felt a little worried about how we were going to handle moving somewhere where another language was spoken.

The next day at school, we were the talk of the playground. Few military families lived this far away from Maxwell Air Force Base in Montgomery, and most of the students were native Alabamians. The thought of crossing an ocean and living where English wasn't the main language was definitely an intriguing thought, even for some of the teachers.

As the months passed, we had a work plan to finish whenever we had spare time from baseball practice, piano and dance lessons. Each of us had to go through our wardrobe and take out clothes which we hadn't worn or didn't fit. Then came the toughest part: deciding on which toys to leave. Now instead of behaving like our dad at home, he became a military officer, Major Miller, barking orders at his family. He was quite specific on who could take what. We weren't very happy with the statement, ". . . some toys will have to stay."

"Mom, why can't I take my Sally Walker doll? I remember when I opened the package on Christmas day in fourth grade at Patrick Air Force Base. No one will have a doll like her in France. Just because she is so big, isn't a reason. I should still be able to take her," I lamented. I couldn't imagine a time when my dolls would not be a part of my life. I played with them almost every day. And now, with Carole Anne a little older, we sometimes played together.

"Sandra, I know this is tough for you; however, we didn't make the rules. A specific weight allowance is part of the move. All our things will be going over on a freighter along with the furniture of other families moving to Europe."

We were sitting at the maple kitchen table, sharing a glass of lemonade as I pleaded my case.

"You'll be twelve in one month and the next year you'll start your teen-age years. Do you really think you'll be playing with dolls then? I haven't had time to tell you the most exciting news of all. When you start high school, you'll go up to Paris and live in a dorm with all the other students from Fontainebleau."

"What do you mean live in a dorm? Why won't I be living at home?" I scrunched up my face in disbelief, focusing my hazel eyes directly into her dark brown eyes. "Why isn't there a school where we are going? How far away will I be?" My fingers shook as I ran them through my short brown hair, pushing my bangs off my forehead. I just couldn't believe this new idea.

"There is a junior high with grades 7-9, but there aren't enough students to justify a separate high school. Most of the students will be coming from other Army posts and Air Force bases around France. Besides, this will prepare you for going away to college." She smiled at me. "You might even be glad to get away from us by then."

My mom patted my shoulder, showing comfort, because she saw the disbelief of a brand new idea, moving away from home.

"No. I won't know anyone. Who will I stay with? Will I get a room by myself?" The questions came like rapid gun-fire as I stood up and grabbed a tissue from the Kleenex box on the kitchen counter to dab the few tears which were starting to form. I felt overwhelmed with what my friends later called 'neat' news.

At school the next day I talked with Miss Hazel who shared with me about going away to college and living in a dorm. She had enrolled at Auburn University a long distance from where she grew up, in the northwest part of the state, a small town called Winfield. After finishing this conversation, I thought I might actually have fun living in a dormitory.

The next few months seemed to fly by with all the preparations for the move. I continued my weekly piano and ballet lessons, Carole Anne finished her tap dance lessons and Harvey was almost able to finish the baseball season. He felt a little sad at having to miss the play-offs, yet at the same time he felt excited about the upcoming trip.

An end of the school year picnic was scheduled. I had to bring pineapple sandwiches for my sixth grade class picnic on the last day of school.

"Mom, do you know how to make these sandwiches? There are sure some weird items on this menu."

"Dear, we'll have this same experience in France. In my French class on base, I found out the French eat *escargot,* 'specially grown snails. Here inn the south, some of the foods we've tried this year weren't available when we lived in New York, Pennsylvania or New Jersey.

"Remember when you ate boiled okra and tomatoes at Grandmother Miller's house, on our last visit to Clearwater?"

"Yuk! I do remember." I frowned. "But snails? I can't imagine what they would taste like. Be sure you learn all the food words so whenever we go out, you'll know what we are eating, okay? I really am not up for surprises when we eat at a French restaurant."

The last day of school arrived and during the final morning recess, I went out to the playground to get some addresses from some of my favorite friends so they could write. Many were happy to know someone who would actually cross the Atlantic Ocean on a huge ship. They kept coming up to get in line to give their addresses.

The sixth grade graduation ceremonies started at four thirty. I felt happy to have my family sitting in the audience because my dad usually missed ceremonies, baseball games and piano recitals. I had picked out a new sleeveless blue dress with lace around the bottom and put on an extra petticoat. For just a short time I felt more grown up, realizing my mom had been right. I would be a teenager in one more year. My sister kept waving to me as I walked across the stage to get my diploma. As I shook the principal's hand, he whispered to me, "Have a great time for all of us."

I returned to my seat and looked around the auditorium at my classmates and friends, most of whom I'd probably never see again.

Mom is right. A new adventure is beginning.

CHAPTER TWO

THE ROLLING SEA

Crossing the Atlantic Ocean

"Look at the size of this boat," my younger brother Harvey exclaimed, using all the fingers on his right hand to point up toward a huge grey boat.

"Now children, I've told you before, this is a military ship, not a boat. We will be living here for the next ten days while we cross the Atlantic to go to France," my dad said with some exasperation in his voice.

"Daddy, I'm not real sure I want to go this, um, ship. Why can't we go a faster way?" My younger sister Carole Anne held onto my hand tightly as she looked up at my dad. She pushed her long blond bangs off her freckled forehead.

I felt a little unsure of this monstrous vessel which would take our family to Europe. As the oldest, at twelve, I worried about my younger brothers and sister. None of us had ever been in anything but a car. I could only imagine how frightening the size of this ship might look to my younger sister, now age seven.

We followed our parents, aunt, uncle and cousin up the long gangplank onto the first deck. Someone in a fancy uniform told my dad how to sign in and where we needed to go to find our rooms. We went through a large door and over to the sign-in-desk. Another man in a military uniform talked about the procedure for finding our luggage.

Everyone walked over to what looked like an open elevator and followed a winding staircase, going down deep into the ship. Our room felt tiny, like a little walk-in closet. There were two sets of metal bunk beds, each set stacked against a wall with a small three drawer dresser in-between. The mattresses were very thin. A set of sheets had been placed on the inside corner of each bed. The pillows felt used too, no fluffy feeling here. A grey metal door opened to an adjoining room for our parents with a double bed, two small dressers, a tiny closet and a very small room which turned out to be the bathroom. Unfortunately, there was no bathtub, only a toilet, a sink and a very narrow shower.

All of us walked back upstairs to say our good-byes to Aunt Vera, Uncle John and fourteen year old cousin, Barbara. As we stood on the wooden deck, I watched two large smoke stacks blow out thick grey and white puffs of smoke. A sharp whistle sound blew signaling our leaving. I wondered what these next few years could bring. I watched the New York harbor slip away from view and felt a little scared. In all of our military transfers, I had never been through anything like this.

We walked carefully around the deck as a gust of wind blew all around us. I held onto my new white sailor hat which I hoped would keep my short brown hair from blowing everywhere. For a summer day, the air felt really chilly. I hoped we wouldn't have any colder weather on the open sea. There wasn't a cloud in the entire pale blue sky, yet the sun didn't warm my shivering legs and arms. I pulled up the zipper on my thin red jacket and said to my brother and sister,

"This will really be fun if we make this an adventure. Remember when we played cowboys and Indians back in Prattville?"

Carole Anne looked up at me and frowned. "What will we do all day? We don't have anything to make costumes here."

We went back inside and walked down the long winding stairs to our room. My dad picked up a large manila envelope placed next to our door and handed it to my mom who sat down on the bed to read it.

She glanced at the papers. "Look at this, a list of places you can go to play. There is a game room, a movie theatre and a gym. Sounds as though someone knows children need to keep busy on a long ocean voyage." She stood up and put Jon in a small crib which had been put inside the tiny closet while we were gone.

At six o'clock, we made our way up to the dining room. On deck, walking straight still seemed difficult. For our first meal, I looked around at all the tables and saw nothing falling off. I had an upset stomach and felt nervous about eating any food, so I just ordered soup, no dinner.

Our good-looking Italian waiter, Antonio, said there would be soup every night as a first course. He had wavy black hair and dark brown eyes. Right away I knew we were in trouble. Harvey, the brave one of us children asked, "What's a first course, mom?"

She explained how the dinner meal had each part served separately, first soup, then salad, then a main course of chicken, fish, or meat and a vegetable and finally dessert. We settled down to see what happened next. Antonio brought a large serving bowl of steaming soup to our table. He served each person by dipping a large ladle into the soup and giving each of us a bowl filled with one scoop of a wonderfully smelling liquid.

I liked the taste immediately because the vegetables were not huge chunks, but tiny pieces. I could swallow them if I didn't like whatever green or white cube appeared on my spoon. About halfway through this first course, Carole Anne said, "I don't feel so good." She covered her mouth and stood up to dash out of the room, loosing her soup just before the doorway. She started crying immediately. "I'm sorry, Mommy."

The head waiter came to our table and showed his sympathy. "Don't worry Madame, your children aren't the only ones to be sick on the first night, and I'm sure they won't be the last. Why don't you put her to bed with some saltine crackers, a little water and a half aspirin? We'll get this mess cleaned up right away."

Luckily, the excitement of the day in a brand new environment and the rolling of the ship put us to sleep right way. We never heard our parents come in, talk or get ready for bed.

The first morning gave us a clear blue sky with a bright sun. The waves were huge with whitecaps making up most of the wave. The wind continued to blow and it felt really cold. We braved walking on the open deck to get to the dining room, holding on to the smooth wooden railing with each hesitating step. The pitching of the ship in the water didn't help my stomach feel any more settled. When we arrived at the dining room, I felt so lucky to have our same good looking waiter, Antonio.

"Mademoiselle, you still look a little green." He picked Carole Anne up and put her in her seat. "A good breakfast is all you need to settle your queasy stomach." She looked up at him in surprise. She didn't expect to get picked up.

There seemed to be over a hundred people in this room. Groups of six to eight people sat at fourteen large round tables, covered with yellow tablecloths and a round bowl filled with yellow and white flowers. By the time we ordered, I didn't feel any better and neither did Carole Anne. She tapped me on the knee.

"What are you going to get?"

"Dad, do we have to eat? We still don't feel so good." Of course he agreed with the waiter and mom.

"The best thing for you young lady would be some food. Why don't you just try some oatmeal, dry toast and milk."

Ugh, I thought to myself. "Dad, this sounds awful."

For some weird reason, my sister and I were able to keep our food down. Ever smiling, Antonio brought a list of choices for lunch and dinner. As I heard the choices, I felt my swelling stomach start to rumble again. "Mom, I'm not feeling so good. Can I leave and find a restroom?"

Antonio pointed the way out of the dining room. I wondered if the rolling of the ship was the only reason I felt so terrible or if maybe it was the food. I returned a few minutes later to see my parents finishing their coffee. By then Harvey looked a little green. He stood up quickly and rushed out of the room as I took my seat.

"Children, do you want peanut butter sandwiches or chicken salad for lunch?"

"Could I have something soft, like scrambled eggs?"

"Now Sandra, you know perfectly well breakfast food shouldn't be eaten at lunch," my dad added. His freckled face showed concern over this idea of eating each meal at the right time, a conversation we had talked about many times.

"Dear, we have eaten breakfast foods at lunch and dinner when you were flying rotations. Maybe something soft will help settle her stomach." My mom showed concern too as she patted my shoulder, smiled and nodded her head.

Carole Anne said, "Daddy, I just don't feel like eating much now. Why do we have to pick our food now?"

After we heard another explanation about the length of time food preparation takes for so many people, I kicked Carole Anne under the table. "Remember, an adventure." I whispered to her as she grimaced at the kick.

Antonio came over to our table and said the ship doctor might have something which would help our seasickness. As soon as everyone finished, we went to the dispensary. He gave us some medicine and tried to comfort us by telling us a lot of adults get seasick too. "This is quite normal for first time passengers. Try to relax these first few days, children. Believe me, the waves won't hurt the ship and we aren't doing to sink."

"How long . . ." I didn't finish my sentence because Jon started crying.

"You should feel better before dinner," he said with confidence.

Harvey asked, "What can we do now?"

"Mom do they have anything just for seven year olds?" Carole Anne looked a little worried. "I don't know anyone, so who will I play with?"

"Let's go over to the gym and see what activities are planned today for your group. They have several choices listed on today's schedule."

We walked into the gym and saw several groups of children playing basketball, ping-pong, jump rope and board games. I decided I should lead the way, so I walked over to a group of girls about my age and asked if I could play jacks with them. Mom put Jon in a playpen in an area for toddlers and went with Carole Anne to find a board game she and Harvey could play. Dad decided to go back to the room and fill out some paperwork, required for entering France.

Somehow the rest of the morning passed and we enjoyed meeting other kids and having something fun to do. In the afternoon they showed a Disney movie and by dinner we were anxious to share our day. Luckily for us, we were scheduled for the first seating at six p.m. The meal of fried chicken, mashed potatoes and green beans actually tasted good. I hoped this meant the medicine worked and I wouldn't get sick after dinner.

The sea seemed rougher than yesterday, with taller waves. We joked a little while watching the water slide from side to side in the glasses. I felt nervous and didn't want to worry my brother or sister. I poked by dad's knee to get his attention, then leaned over to him and whispered, "Dad, is everything okay? We sure seem to be tossing a lot more than yesterday."

He leaned over to me and patted my arm. "Don't worry, Sandra. Everything is under control. We are almost in the middle of the Atlantic Ocean and this is expected. Open sea isn't always calm. Maybe in the next decade or two someone will figure out how to make a ship glide through the water."

As each day began, we learned how to relax while walking on deck and how to pretend sliding and bending over a little would be like flying down a roller coaster ride at top speed. Somehow we stood on deck a little better each day, grasping the rails tightly and moved with the ship. By walking at a slant on the outside deck we made our way to the dining room three times a day without falling.

Some of the meals were never as delicious as Mom's. We did learn how to appreciate different tastes and styles of cooking as well as eat food we'd never had before. Because of these choices, I realized what a good cook my mom had been. Here I had no choice but to eat what would be served to me three times a day.

The daily activities kept us busy and playing with other children helped pass the time. We survived the ten day crossing and had no other problems. First we stopped at Southampton, England, for some passengers to get off. After we docked at Bremerhaven, Germany, we boarded a non-stop train for Paris to begin the next phase of my dad's military tour, overseas: a new adventure in a new country.

CHAPTER THREE
WHAT'S THIS?

Paris, France, 1957

"Can you believe we are really here?" my younger sister Carole Anne asked. Her green eyes were shinning with delight as she looked at the country style décor outside the French restaurant. We were getting ready to eat our first lunch in France.

"Mom, what kind of food do they have here . . .I'm really hungry . . .we had only those weird shaped rolls at breakfast." My younger brother Harvey rambled on and Carole Anne interrupted him.

I looked at both of them. "Come on, don't start making a big deal. Can't you wait a little longer?"

My mother looked from one child's smiling face to another's grumpy one as she tried to answer all concerns at once. When the concierge at our hotel had recommended this place, she seemed a little nervous since her French had been learned in twelve 'easy' lessons.

This was our first full day in France and even though I was the oldest, at twelve, I felt nervous too. "Mom, let me hold Jon for a minute."

Breakfast had been included with our hotel rooms. We had hoped for an American breakfast of cereal or eggs. Instead, we had tender brioche and flaky croissant rolls with little butter curls and delicious apricot jam. As good as these rolls tasted, they really did not fill us up. We wanted Cheerios. When the hot chocolate came to our

20

table in extra large cups, there seemed to be something missing. My seven year old little sister seemed to be the only one noticing a difference when she exclaimed, "Where's the marshmallows?"

Our dad had called the hotel to say he wouldn't be able to meet us for lunch. The initial paperwork to get us settled into France and his routine job duties for this overseas Air Force assignment were going to delay him through lunch. My mom had been studying French for about three months, so she told us not to worry. "I can read a menu, kids. We're set."

At noon we arrived at this quaint little house easily with the directions we were given by the hotel concierge. All of us continued to stare at the stucco building as though we were waiting for someone to invite us inside.

My mom finally spoke. "Come on children, we've been to restaurants before. Let's just enjoy this new experience."

My eleven year old brother finally broke the tension by asking, "Are we going to stand here or go in and eat?"

Carole Anne gently punched him in the ribs whispering, "You'd better be good."

The worn wooden door opened from the inside and two well dressed men, wearing pin striped suits and colorful ties walked out into the bright Parisian sunshine. I looked at the large red geraniums planted in the window box and wondered out loud, "Can't we eat outside?" Most of the tables were full.

When I turned around, everyone had already gone inside. I shifted Jon to my other hip as I walked into a beautifully decorated room and stared in amazement. The room was fancier than the plain façade of beige stucco indicated. We stared at the white starched tablecloths covering the round tables. Each held a perfect red rose in a clear glass vase in the middle of the table.

A short thin man wearing a white shirt, red bow tie and black jacket stood behind a wooden podium. He looked at us with questions. His black pants had a perfectly ironed crease down the middle and his dark shoes were shinning. His black wavy hair was slicked back and his pencil thin moustache fit all the recent images I had pictured in my mind of a Frenchman.

« Bonjour Madame. Voulez-vous une table toute de suite ou est-ce que vous attendez quelqu'un ? »

I could see my mom's perfectly shaped brown eyebrows scrunch up, probably translating in her head. She bent down to us, whispering. "I think he's asking us if we want a table now or are we waiting for someone. Maybe he thinks we are waiting for your dad. I'll tell him we are ready to be seated."

She spoke ever so slowly. I saw his thin black eyebrows move up and down on his forehead as a smile slowly appeared. In a heavily accented voice he replied in perfect English, "Of course Madame. Please follow me."

When we arrived at our table, we were seated next to a large picture window which showed us a little *jardin des fleurs*, (flower garden) filled with different sizes of tall green plants and many flowers in a variety of colors. Part of the view had been obscured by a beautiful white lace curtain hanging over part of the cracked windowpane.

Carole Anne spoke first. "Mom, what's all this extra silverware?"

At my place there were three forks turned over to the left of a large white china plate bordered with blue and white checks; in the middle of this plate a white napkin had been folded like a pleated fan. The knife and spoon were face-up in their usual place. My brother asked, "Why is there a large spoon turned over at the top of my plate Mom. How come I have three glasses?"

"Remember what we talked about before we left the hotel? Eating habits are different here, so take a minute and observe how the others are eating," Mom said quietly as she looked at the small table next to ours, seating four businessmen in navy blue suits.

After cutting their food, instead of putting down the knife and switching the fork to the right hand, the other customers ate with the fork still in the left hand, turned over. My brother and sister seemed fascinated. He said, "Wow, would you look . . . they don't switch hands. Sure looks easier, Mom. Can we eat the same way?"

She answered yes, and we continued to watch while trying hard not to stare. Our waiter seemed to appear out of nowhere and my first thought was he must not have missed many meals. His broad grin drew my attention to rosy round cheeks. A spotless white apron was around his ample waist and his long thick brown hair had been tied behind his neck with some type of cord. After greeting us with a sentence in French, "*Bonjour Madame, Etes-vous prêt?*" (Good day, Ma'am. Are you ready?) He started to hand out four menus.

I saw Mom take a deep breath and say: "*Non monsieur, seulement moi.*" (No sir, only me.) He only gave her the menu, a large blue rectangular shaped card. Mom looked at this menu very carefully saying, "Be patient a minute, children. I must read each line before I can tell you what they have. So far, I recognize the words chicken, fish, soup, salad, cheese and fruit. Some of the proper names might describe how the food is cooked or they might have a special meaning. I'm not sure of a couple of items."

We were all a little anxious, so Carole Anne casually mentioned, "I just wanted a hamburger and fries," as she nervously twisted a strand of blond hair around her finger.

Then Harvey asked, "Do they have *poulet* (fried chicken)?"

"Children, please, wait a minute. Maybe our waiter can help out with the translation."

Mom told him we were ready to order if he would answer a couple of questions. As the conversation progressed, she told us she thought there might have been some difficulty either in his translation or her comprehension.

She smiled bravely, I thought, pushing some black curls off her forehead, as she said: "We're adventurous today, right? I'm quite sure of most of the items. Let's either try something new and different or go with the words I know for sure."

Right away my sister and brother made a face. "I don't want to eat something I don't like," Carole Anne said, her face showing her concern with creases on her forehead and a frown on her face. Harvey continued, ". . . 'cause if the taste isn't good, I'll have to eat everything on my plate, just like at home. This isn't fair, Mom."

"I'll only order two entrées and you can share. This way if we don't like the meal, we won't waste much. If you're still hungry, maybe we can find a hot dog stand later." This seemed to settle everyone down, so she proceeded to order, speaking very slowly.

First came a bowl of steaming vegetable broth filled with carrots, celery and onion, peas and yellow squash, all cut in tiny pieces. Our waiter ladled the soup into our bowls from a large blue tureen. Then he put a slice of REAL French bread on our plate and added a curl of off-white butter. This butter tasted different. I found out from Mom there was no salt added. The bread was crispy outside, soft and chewy inside . . . delicious. Then he brought a salad with only curly and red lettuce, covered with a-just-right combination of oil and vinegar.

"How come there's only lettuce on the plate?" My mom made a face. She said she forgot a French salad is only lettuce. "If you want any raw vegetables, you must order them."

When the main course arrived, we were served from a large platter filled with parsley covered roasted red potatoes, green beans and thin slices of beef covered with a yellow sauce. I dipped one finger into the sauce and tasted a spicy mustard flavor. The first bite of meat should have been my clue, yet I was going to be adventurous today so I took a second smaller bite.

"This meat tastes a little salty, and the texture's a little chewy, kinda like a pot roast not cooked right," I said hesitantly. I looked at my mom and spoke bravely. "You try some Mom. What kind of meat is this?"

As she tasted her bite, Mom's mouth puckered a little; she said "The sauce is quite good, but I don't recognize the meat's flavor or grainy texture. We can ask out waiter later. These green beans are quite good. If you clean your plates you have a choice of fruit, cheese or pastry for dessert."

"I only want chocolate ice cream," my brother said defiantly, picking up his spoon and tapping it on the table. "At least I'll have one god thing to eat from this lunch." His freckled face showed quite an unhappy scowl.

"Who would want fruit and cheese for dessert?" Carole Anne asked.

"Mom, I'd like to try a real French pastry," I added, dreaming of chocolate and whipped cream.

"Since we can't seem to agree, we'll skip dessert today." Mom had decided for all of us. She looked around for our waiter.

"It's your fault. Now we don't get anything," my brother grimaced as he kicked at Carole Anne under the table. Jon continued to eat small pieces of bread and green beans.

After the bill arrived, Mom hesitantly asked the waiter to name the type of beef we had, as we were unfamiliar with the taste. She spoke slowly and carefully, but he shrugged his shoulders and looked up, just as the Maitre D' happened to be walking by our table. He was able to help translate and replied with pride how happy he was to have served one of the house favorites, ordered frequently by the local patrons, to such a nice American family. Then he complimented mom on her efforts to speak French when she ordered our food.

He told her there were few families who came to this restaurant, much less Americans, since they were not located on a main street. She told him how much we enjoyed the décor, and the food. She told him she had just one specific question about out meal. I noticed how carefully she spoke each word. Since I didn't speak French, every word she said sounded just beautiful to me. I hoped we'd get a chance to have French as one of our classes at the junior high. When she mentioned another cut of beef, he replied with a question, smiling.

"Madame, didn't you know you ordered cow's tongue?"

CHAPTER FOUR

MY OWN SPACE

Bois-le-Roi, France, 1957

My younger brother, sister and I shared a bedroom for many years. When our youngest brother Jon was born, I figured out I would never get to have any privacy, much less a room of my own. When we were all little, sometimes it was nice not to be alone at night when all the strange house noises occurred, but as I grew older, I needed my own space.

When my dad received an overseas assignment, this seemed like the icing on the cake for a career Air Force pilot. I remembered our conversation:

"Well, I have the orders in my hand and I wonder who can guess where we're going? Each of you gets only one pick," my dad said.

"Too late, Dad. We already guessed with Mom after we came home from school this afternoon," Carole Anne answered. "We just couldn't wait 'til you came home."

"Then you know we're going to Germany?" he responded with a grin.

"Oh no, Mom. You said we were going to France. I was really looking forward to eating real French bread," I answered.

"Well, Sandra, I was kidding. You are right. We are going to France."

None of us knew what was in store for our family after we had crossed the Atlantic Ocean, eaten our first meal in a French restaurant and then drove to the little town of Bois-le-Rois, about a 20 minute drive from Fountainebleau, the town where my dad would be working for the next three years.

We turned off the main road and saw a beautiful large stone house built on a very big lot with a long rectangular green lawn in front, many small trees and shrubs planted around the house. There was a huge stone wall next to the road and a black wrought iron fence built into this wall which surrounded the house. At the time, I had no way of knowing this would be my home for the next four years.

"Wow, can you believe this house has three stories? And look at the neat balconies going across the front on the first two floors," Harvey exclaimed. "We sure can play some neat games, and even have room to build forts up there."

"Children, before you get any wild ideas remember: we are only renting. This house belongs to someone else. We must take extra care not to damage anything." My dad responded with a stern voice.

"Dad, we're just going to play, like we did in our back yard in Prattville. You don't have to worry," eleven year old Harvey replied.

As he unlocked the gate, pushed open one side and came back inside the car, I looked up at the large stone tower on the back side of the house. As we drove inside the back yard I asked, "What do you suppose this is, Dad?"

"Sandra you'll be quite interested in the history of this house. This tower encloses the stairs going up to each level of the house. At the top is a small room which the Germans used during WWII to look out over the neighboring area. This house is bordered by the King's Forest, which is the translation of the town, Bois-wood, le-the

Roi– King. Hundreds of years ago kings hunted here regularly. In Fountainebleau, where I will be working, is a beautiful palace built in the 16th century by Francis I. Down the street about a mile, is the famous Seine River.”

“Can you believe we’re not only getting to live in a neat looking place, but now we can find out some great stuff for our history reports,” I said to Harvey. “Dad, how do you know all this history?”

When I went to junior college, I studied European history and I remembered some of what I learned about France. You will be able to have some great information to put in your reports as you learn more about this area.”

Inside, we literally raced from floor to floor, trying to find which space would be our bedrooms. I couldn’t believe I’d finally get to have the peace and quiet I’d always wanted.

On the second floor, Harvey stopped at the first door and pushed slowly. It opened into what looked like a tiny closet. “Will you look here; a toilet, and a weird one too. Why is there a big bowl on top and a long chain with a handle at the bottom?”

“Who cares?” Carole Anne answered, as she quickly pushed slowly on the next door which opened to a hallway with a large bedroom on the left and double French doors going out to the balcony. The next room was another bedroom with the same type of doors opening onto the balcony. “I sure don’t want my room next to Mom and Dad’s,” she yelled to us as we entered the bathroom.

"Double wow," I said as I walked over to a large white bathtub with four claw feet. There was also a sink and another weird shaped toilet. "Hey Mom, what kind of toilet is this thing?"

"All right children, just stop where you are," Mom answered as she came down the hall with Jon on her hip. She stopped, put him down and said, "Remember when I talked about an adventure? Some things are different here. This bathroom is a great example. If you'll just hold on for a minute, I'll explain."

"I want to see what's on the top floor," Carole Anne said as she turned around to leave.

"Wait just one minute, young lady," Mom replied sternly. "Do you want answers to your questions or do you want to explore this house?"

"We want to see the rest of the house," Harvey said as Carole Anne and I nodded in agreement.

"Can you tell us when we finish, Mom?"

Six feet climbed the curving staircase quickly until they reached the third floor. Harvey opened the first door yelling, "This one is mine. I want this room."

My sister ran to the second, smaller room with a dormer window and proclaimed, "This one is mine. I want this one."

With only one door left, I walked wistfully down the narrow hall ever so slowly. I wondered what would be on the other side of this worn wooden door. When I peeked into the room, I just couldn't believe my good luck. This was the largest of the three rooms, the only one with wallpaper, and not just any old paper . . . beautifully painted blue wild flowers. A tiny balcony with a black wrought iron railing outside the French doors was my only window on the wall which sided on the street. In the corner was yet another door opening to a small room with a sink, a window in the ceiling and the same kind of weird toilet as downstairs. The room even smelled fresh as though someone had just gone over every part of the room with some kind of neat smelling perfumed cleanser.

I just stood there with my mouth open when my brother and sister wandered into my room, both saying at the same time, "I want this room."

As the sound of their voices became louder, Mom finally arrived at the top of the staircase holding Jon's hand as he practiced his new found skill of walking.

"Children, come here!" she said sternly, again. After hearing all sides, she agreed with me. The selection process picked at the beginning was to stand. The bedroom each picked first was to be the room kept.

I closed the door to my own space and surveyed the furniture. A large wood armoire was in one corner. Inside there were five shelves, two drawers and a metal rod for hanging clothes. On the other wall was a large wooden box which, I found out later, folded down into a double bed. Included in this hide-a-bed was a single book shelf under the opening with an enclosed shelf on each end as well as a built-in light under the bookshelf. Was I in heaven or what?

Carole Anne called out to me, "Sandy can you come in here?"

I walked into her room and saw another wooden box. We pulled a handle and a single bed came out, with a bookshelf and a light. There was a small dresser in the other corner and a neat wicker rocking chair in the other. A small bench with a long patchwork cushion of blue and white squares fit under the dormer window. Her freckled face scrunched up in confusion.

"See, you have a neat room too, Carole Anne. You sit here, read or just look out the window. If you put pictures on the walls, you can get some color in here and make this be your own space." Her green eyes sparkled as she nodded in agreement.

"Yeah, I do like this room 'cause if I had a larger room like yours I'd have to take more time to clean everything. Thanks for helping me with the bed. Won't this be neat? We can have friends over to spend the night too."

When the moving van finally arrived two months later, I unpacked my carefully chosen stuffed animals and dolls. I arranged them on top of the shelf of my new bed, animals first then my two dolls. My dressing table was nothing more than two end tables covered with a ruffled blue tablecloth and a glass top. I set this up on the only remaining empty wall. As I put my lamp on this table, I felt truly at home in my own space, even though I was thousands of miles from my friends back in the states.

What would these next years bring, as I stepped out of my childhood into my teens, here in France? I had high hopes for growing up here. Now I had my own space to dream, ponder and wish for whatever I might find as I ventured down this un-chartered path for my life. Here on foreign soil I would probably experience my first kiss, my first boyfriend, and maybe even my first love.

Let the adventure begin.

\

CHAPTER FIVE

WHAT ARE YOU SAYING?

Bois-le-Roi, France, 1958

As I sat in my straightbacked uncomfortable wood *chaise* (chair) behind a squared off table in the first row, I could feel the tears start to form in my eyes. I squirmed, then scratched my arm while trying to muster up the courage *lever* (to stand) and face them.

My new *maitre* (teacher) repeated my name with an accent. I guess she told them to welcome me, the new American student, because they all said "BONJOUR" at the same time. I finally pushed the chair back, turned around slowly and muttered "Hello" to the blur of faces in this eighth grade class, *classe de cinquieme des filles* (fifth class of girls) in Bois-le-Roi, France.

The silence had been interrupted by giggling because I spoke in English, so I sat down quickly, wondering how I'd ever manage to learn anything here.

" 'ere is your notebook, your ink pen, your textboook and your inkwell," said my teacher matter-of-factly. Luckily for me *la pupitre* (the desk) I moved to was in the back of the room, away from the rest of the worn old-fashioned wooden school desks. I put my bottle of *encre* (ink) into the well and wondered how I'd learn to write with this metal nib. I had never seen one of these pointed old fashioned pens before, and I felt worried. How would I get the ink to flow correctly on a page of paper?

My new teacher looked like my idea of an old maid. She had short tight curly brown hair and wire rimmed glasses. She wore a dull beige sweater with a dark tan skirt which came down well below her knees. She spoke French rapidly, using her hands. I couldn't help but notice how well kept they were. *Ses ongles* (Her fingernails) were short, but just long enough to see a small white tip which had been filed to a point. *Ses doigts* (Her fingers) were stubby and she wore no rings. Instead, I saw a small tan leather wrist band surrounding a plain silver *montre* (watch) on her bony right wrist. She wore the kind of *souliers* (shoes) I would have imagined my great grandmother wearing in her old age: like short boots going up above her ankles, straight-laced, rounded at the toes, dull brown, with only a trace of a well worn heal on both shoes.

I wondered how my sister survived in her class, across the hall. Just then *une sonnett* (a bell) rang. I gathered from the motions my teacher made with her hands, this would be a recess. I searched for my little sister who seemed to be overwhelmed by a circle of eight year old girls, all talking to her at the same time.

"Carole Anne, over here," I yelled. Although she didn't talk to anyone, all those around her pointed at me as she walked away.

"Hi Sandy. How terrible is your teacher?"

"You couldn't have one worse than mine."

"Oh yes I could. Remember, you are older so you probably have someone with experience. My teacher looks like one of the girls in your class. I bet she's a brand new teacher. Does yours speak English?"

"A little. What do you suppose these girls think of us coming here? I just don't see how this can work. I have no idea what she is saying and she never said a word about speaking English when I showed her I didn't understand the directions she gave."

I shoved my hands into the deep *poches* (pockets) of my blue smock, a requirement for attending this French school. It looked like a lightweight extra large shirt, covering your clothes, going down about halfway on your skirt.

"What should we do?" Carole Anne looked perplexed. "I think some of the girls from my class want me to play jump rope, but when I heard you call my name, I just ran to you. How do you think our brother is doing?"

"Let's go over to the dividing wall and see if he's out there," I suggested.

We walked over to the large broken rock *mur (* wall) dividing the girls section from the boys. We saw our brother standing alone in the playground. He looked as sad as we felt, eyebrows scrunched, wearing a frown on his face. I called his name as someone called mine.

"Harvey, can you come over here?"

"Mademoiselle Sandra. Mademoiselle Carole Anne." We heard our names and turned around to see a large heavy set *femme* (woman) walk up to us. She grabbed our arms and pulled us away from the barrier as our brother arrived. "Guess we'll have to talk later," Carole Anne called back to him as he stood there waving good-bye.

We felt stuck in a corner as this woman rattled off a long string of words in a tone which made me guess we weren't allowed to talk with boys. I shrugged my shoulders as did Carole Anne. "Do you think she knows we don't understand?"

« Oh, *les Américaines* » were the only words I caught. She wasn't pleased with us, as she pointed a finger at the boys and shook it back and forth as if to tell us no.

"I hope we can sit together at lunch," my sister mentioned as everyone else lined up to go back inside.

As soon as we sat down, the other students started doing math problems at their desks. I watched carefully as some wrote problems on the board. Their numbers were written differently. The number one had a long line in front and the number *sept* (seven) had a line through the straight long line. I tried to figure out what they were doing and decided a little later this must be beginning algebra.

« *Il faut travailler.* » (One must work). She pointed to the paper and my pen, making motions for me to write down the numbers written on the board.

Once again, I shrugged my shaking shoulders while my knees shook under the desk. I looked up into her thin face and said as politely as possible, "I don't understand anything you are saying."

The next class didn't go any better, but at least I recognized *une carte* (a map) of the United States. This must be a Geography class. I continued to listen to these new sounds, but couldn't answer any questions or talk to anyone.

At lunch time, we were pleased to find everyone going home for lunch. As we walked around the narrow curve on the dirt path behind the main road toward our house, Harvey said, "I hate this place.

How do you think we can get out of this crazy idea of dad's to learn French by getting put in this school?"

Both Carole Anne and I shrugged our shoulders out of habit from the first morning round of questions from our teachers. We continued to walk home in silence, each probably lost in our own thoughts.

Mom greeted us at the door with a cheery, "*Bonjour*. Welcome home for your first *déjeuner (*lunch). Three shaky voices said almost at the same time, "We hate this school."

During the hour long lunch break I tried to come up with a plan. Mom said she would talk to dad after we went to bed. She smiled at us, "Be brave, remember, this is a great adventure." I knew she referred to our first lunch in a French restaurnant when she ordered cow's tongue by mistake. I hoped she'd come up with some sort of plan, fast.

Somehow I managed to get through the long afternoon.My head started to ache after *la seconde classe* (second class) back from lunch, since the sounds I had to listen to made no sense to me at all. Once in a while, a student would point to something in an effort *aider* (to help) me. For the most part I sat alone, as if hidden by a thick fog.

During afternoon recess, I noticed how clear and bright *le ciel* (the sky) had become, no clouds anywhere. Several large green *arbres* (trees) shaded a corner of the playground which was only dirt. I walked over there and sat down, smelling the fragrance of a neighbor's colorful flowers next to the wooden fence. I waved to my sister who jumped rope with a group of second graders. The toe of my right shoe seemed to dig a small hole in the dirt. I picked up the brown sandy textured dirt and let the grains sift slowly through my fingers, two of them covered in black ink.

I wondered what my friends were doing back at the junior high in Fountainbleau, where I had gone last year as a seventh grader.

For an entire week the three of us struggled through seven classes a day, hoping against all odds this would soon end. At dinner one *vendredi soir* (Friday night), three sad faces looked at our dad again, as I started a familiar conversation. Jon played quietly in his high chair, oblivious to our predicament.

"Just reconsider, Dad. You can't imagine how terrible a situation can be when no one tells you what's going on," I said bravely. As the oldest, I felt I had to get this argument started now or we'd have another treacherous trial again next week, with our teachers acting as judge and jury.

"Daddy, can't we have someone tell us in English what we are supposed to do?" Carole Anne started crying. "I want to go back home to the United States."

Dead silence.

My dad looked at my mom who shook her head up and down, indicating approval. She looked at us with a broad smile.

"Fine. I've heard enough. Your mother will arrange for a private tutor *trois* (three) days *une semaine* (a week) after school so you can start learning some vocabularly."

CHAPTER SIX

BACK TO THE JUNIOR HIGH

Bois-le-Roi, France, 1959

After one full year in French schools (half a year in the local school and the other half in a private girl's school in another town), I felt ready to go back to the American junior high on the nearby army post. My younger brother, sister and I had been patient with our dad. He had this weird idea we would learn French by going to local schools. Even he had to face it . . . this just wasn't working.

"Dad, I'll be starting high school this fall and will be behind since I missed eighth grade English, civics and math. I did improve my French, but we studied stuff only in French. I didn't understand a lot of the concepts." I tried to keep my voice calm.

My brother Harvey chimed in," She's right. We tried your idea and this just isn't working. We hate these schools. Pleeze . . . won't you change your mind?"

Mom, always the mediator, stepped up to the plate for at least the third time this week. All of us hoped there would not be a strike out today. I stood next to my sister Carole Anne looking over at our dad who sat on the couch with an exasperated look on his face. Harvey sat on the floor playing with Jon and some Lincoln Logs.

"Dear, don't you agree the children have a valid point about getting ready for our return to the states next year? I know we agreed about the importance of them learning French. They have done well this past year. But the drive to take them to town every morning and then go back to pick them up is difficult. Jon still needs an afternoon nap. A school bus will come to our door, pick them up and bring them home. The private schools are taking a toll on our budget too. We must start thinking about our return to the states."

The fall of 1959 brought a most startling change as our dad, Major Miller reluctantly agreed to let the girls return to the American school on the army post in Fontainebleau, about a 25 minute drive away. Unfortunately for Harvey, his year was going to be spent in the same private boy's school but as a boarder.

Needless to say, I felt overjoyed at the prospect of returning to the junior high and re-kindling former friendships. This past year in French schools had been difficult when it came to meeting my friends. At least there had been one exception. Some of my friends from the junior high lived in Bois-le-Roi.

« Ici Bois-le-Roi deux cent quatre vingt dix-huit. Je voudrais Bois-le-Roi vingt- six. » (This is King's woods 298, I want King's woods, 26) After the operator connected me, I waited nervously to see who would answer. I still felt uncomfortable speaking to an operator.

"Major Burn's residence, Jill speaking."

"Hi Jill, is Linda there?"

"Yeah, hold on. Linda, phone for you. It's Sandy."

"Hi. Haven't heard from you in a while."

"I know. We just returned from a two week family vacation, camping with the Mueller's and Vitteck's in Italy. Wait 'til you hear some really neat news."

42

"What is it? Don't make me wait."

"I get to come back for ninth grade. I'm so happy I can hardly wait for three more weeks 'til school starts."

"Wow, I mean double wow! Hey Jill, Sandy gets to come back to school with me this year. She says hunky dorey. When can you come over so I can tell you all about the new kids?"

"I'll have to ask my mom. Hold on. She said I could ride my bike over, so I'll be there in a few minutes."

"Great. See you then, *Au revoir*." (good bye)

As I went down the gravel pathway on my bike, I took my time. Around the corner from our *maison* (house), the smell of a freshly baked lemon tart floated in the air. Madame Wagon had just put this on her window sill. I waved to my former babysitter who was working in her small vegetable *jardin (*garden). As I came around the corner, I realized when school started in the fall I'd never have to take this road again to attend *Ecole pour les filles* (school for girls).

I rode through an opened wrought iron gate and walked up to the beige stucco two story *maison* (house). The door opened before I could ring the bell.

"Come on in," Linda said as a wide grin spread over her freckled face. "I just can't believe your dad finally gave in." She tightened her red pony tail and closed the door. "This will be such a great year. One of the new things we get to do is have co-ed Physical Education class."

"Wow, what luck. Now I'll get to see guys all day long. Did I ever tell you at the school in town boys and girls are separated?"

"Yeah, you told me. How un-cool," Linda replied. Jill came into her room to boast how this year, as a tenth grader, she'd be riding the bus up to Paris and staying in a dorm at Paris American High School. Her long black hair had been tied with a red ribbon.

"Cool. You guys are so lucky. Getting to go to school in Paris will be such a blast. My dad's tour is over after this year, and I'll never get to go up there." For once, I actually thought of staying another year instead of returning to the states.

"We thought the same thing 'til our dad extended his tour one year," Jill replied. "We didn't know he had such a chance. When we talked 'bout this neat opportunity, everyone said they wanted to stay." She rolled over on the bed, stretching her 5'8'' frame, and grabbing a blue and white checked pillow to put under her head.

"Rats. I wish my dad would do the same thing; but I know there is just no chance. He's so mean to us sometimes. We'd never get to be in such a discussion. Even if we did by some miracle, he wouldn't stay for sure if he knew we wanted to."

"Are you guys still having to prepare your nightly reports for dinner conversation?" Linda asked just as Jill was leaving.

"Nightly reports for dinner? What do you mean?" Jill came back into Linda's room and plopped down on the bed again, looking at Sandy with surprise.

"Oh come on, Jill; don't you remember how we talked about this weird idea last year?" Her younger sister rolled her bright blue eyes to show her exasperation.

"No, I don't. You're right, what a crazy thing to do at dinner."

"You guys are so lucky. My dad is so tough on us about having to speak correctly. He says what we say reflects on him, so by preparing a five minute talk on a specific subject every night we'll not only be ready for speech class in high school, but people will know we are the children of an officer who raised his children to speak right, I mean correctly."

Jill replied, "I sure feel sorry for you. I don't see how I could be studying stuff everyday and then in the summer too."

"Yeah, well he never lets up either. He's been on this as long as I can remember. I was always getting corrected and punished for making mistakes when I spoke. So I finally gave up and figured out maybe I could be ahead of the game when I finally did get to high school." Linda watched as I stood up and went over to the rocking chair to rock back and forth, maybe as a tension relief.

A week later we were told we'd be going to the Army post to sign up for school. Since the process would take a while, we were promised a burger and fries at the snack bar if our behavior was exemplary.

Carole Anne, Jon and Harvey sat in the back seat of the blue Renault and I sat up front with mom. Even though I thought my idea might not work, I decided to try and convince mom to see if dad might consider extending his tour of duty in France. They had been unusually busy this past week with company for dinner one night and a required cocktail party at the Army Post on another night. The car had barely turned the corner onto the main road when a loud pop sounded and the car swerved right.

"Hold on children; we might have a flat tire," my mom managed to say as she pulled off the road. Sure enough, the back tire was flat.

My sister asked. "Mommy, do you know how to change a flat tire on a French car?"

"Well, I've never had this happen before, so everybody get out. We'll see what we can do. Carole Anne, you hold Jon and the rest of you will have to help me figure this out as soon as I find the instruction booklet." She opened the glove compartment.

"Carole Anne, stay away from the road's edge. Please go over to the big rock and sit with Jon."

"Mom, I found the booklet in the back pocket of the front seat," Harvey said, "but all the words are in French. These directions are stuff we never learned in school."

After several minutes of frustration, my mom realized she couldn't translate all the words either.

"Why didn't I ever ask your father how to change a tire after we bought this car?" She looked frazzled as she ran her red manicured fingernails through her short curly black hair in frustration.

"The way to lift up this car is different from the Buick's. I don't see where to place . . ." Her words trailed off. I saw a look of despair on her face, wrinkled with concern.

Suddenly a car door slammed shut. Five pairs of eyes looked behind the Renault to see a heavy set man walking towards them.

« Madame, y-a-t-il un problème ? Ah, oui, je le vois. Je peux vous aider. » (Is there a problem ? Ah, I can see it. I can help you.)

« *Oui monsieur. Vous êtes très gentil. Je ne peut pas le changer.* " (Yes sir, you are very kind. I cannot change it.)

Everyone stood silently as he changed the tire quickly.

« *C'est fini. Bonne chance Madame.* » (It's finished; good luck.)

« *Merci mille fois, Monsieur. Donnez- moi votre numéro de téléphone, s'il vous plait.* » (Thanks a million sir; give me your phone number please.)

« *Mais non, ce n'est pas nécessaire. C'était mon plaisir. Au revoir.* » (Not necessary; my pleasure. Good-bye.) He pushed his sleeves down, buttoned the cuffs and drove off.

We opened the doors and stepped up, inside the car as our mom said, "Well, we certainly were lucky. He was so kind and refused to give us his phone number. I know your dad would have given him something as a thank you."

We arrived at the junior high and I signed up for my classes and had to use my formal name Sandra. Then we went over to the elementary building and signed up Carole Anne. The treat came at the snack bar where we had our favorite lunch of burgers and fries. Then we were off to the boy's school. Harvey lamented his fate of having to live in a dormitory with other French boys, seven days a week. One of the weird things about their school: they had Thursday off and went to school on Saturday.

The big day finally arrived. My sister and I could hardly wait for the school bus to stop at our house. The ride was un-eventful and nerves were a little frayed as the bus came closer to the schools. Carole Anne waved good-bye to me as she walked bravely toward the two story elementary school, which was caddy-corner from the single story junior high. A Quonset hut stood in the middle of the playground area and I wondered why this military building was on school grounds.

I walked ever so slowly into the brick building bustling with students who were swarming the halls shouting familiar greetings and slamming shut locker doors. I felt a little nervous while I found my way to the ninth grade class and cautiously picked a desk in back, folding down my white bobby socks. I put my purse under the desk. Thank goodness I could dress like everyone else and not have to wear a smock over my clothes like I had been required to do in the French schools. My saddle oxfords had been polished and my petticoats starched so my skirt stood out full and wide. I even put clear polish on my nails and curled my short brown hair. I recognized only a few faces and Linda's was one of them. "Hey Linda, come over here."

Linda made her way through the aisles and the bell rang.

Steve Hines said, "What do we have here? Has our little French student returned? Hey there, Mademoiselle Sandra. Did you miss me a lot last year?" He had really shot up since seventh grade. He now stood almost six feet tall. His black wavy hair reminded me of the latest heart throb, a new singer named Elvis Presley.

"You know I want to be called Sandy," I whispered. Before I could comment any more I heard a welcoming phrase. Our new teacher spoke to her 28 new ninth grade students.

"My name is Miss Glover and I'm from Ten Mile, Tennessee, a graduate of the University of Tennessee." Her words slurred in a strong southern drawl as Steve remarked to us, "We sure have a cutie this year."

"Mr. Hines, you will not speak until spoken to. Understood?"

"Yes ma'am. I'm really liking your accent."

"Quite enough, Mr. Hines. Are you ready to spend your first day with our new principal?"

"No ma'am. Sorry." He turned around and winked at us.

She had been in France less than a month. Her long straight brown hair and bangs practically covered her tan face. She went through the first day's schedule and continued to remind all those who interrupted her they would spend their first day with the new principal if they continued to talk while she talked. Everyone's attention went to her as she brought up a new term: 'social schedule'.

When the bell for homeroom ended, Linda said, "Can you believe we're going to have a dance a month? This year hasn't even started and I'm already wondering who will ask me as their date or if we'll all go stag. Maybe I can get a new dress. Can you come to these dances, Sandy?"

"I can't even imagine such luck. With the schedule we have, I'm going to be behind before we start. I missed pre-Algebra, Civics and English grammar from last year, so I'm sure I'll be studying in my spare time. Hopefully French will be my easy class."

"Are you going to take Algebra then? Last year the introduction class was really hard. Didn't you take Algebra in French school?"

"*Mais non*, I didn't. Rats. If I have to add another class I'll really need help. Will you be able to study with me?"

"Sure. Let's go find our Geography *salle* (room). I sure hope we have Mr. Sims again this year, and not another new teacher. He was one of the teachers I really liked because he really helped us learn."

The first *mois* (month) passed quickly as I settled into the new schedule of going to my classes, each with another teacher. In French school, I only had one teacher for all subjects and they never switched rooms. With the adjustment to larger classes, and both *garçons* (boys) and *filles* (girls) in the same class, there were lots of new students to meet. By the time the first social came, I felt worried and happy at the same time. Since the dance would be during the last hour of class, no one could change clothes and we were unhappy with this change of plans from the principal.

My mom asked about the dance as soon as I came home.

"The dance was okay I guess. After the boys picked partners all the wall-flowers choose each other so they'd have someone to dance with. I didn't know the new dance, but I learned quickly from Linda and Steve. The next social will be a hayride; do you think Dad will let me go? I'll need to bring a picnic dinner for me and my date."

"Well, this will be a first step in your social life, dear. I'll certainly go to bat for you. Who will chaperone and where will you go, on the post?" My mom put her arm around me, giving me a hug.

"Mom, I don't know anything yet. Miss Glover said a letter will be coming out for the parents soon with all the information."

The early fall brought a slight chill in the air and a lot of girls were getting worried when they had not been asked to the hayride by the end of September. The date had been set for the second Saturday of October and going through the motions of paying attention in class was becoming more and more difficult for those who didn't have a date.

"Mom, Fred Ferrarie asked me to go to the hayride; did you ask Dad if I could go? I really want to, and Linda said I could spend the night with her so Dad wouldn't have to come pick me up." I looked at my mom, hoping she would have the right answer.

"Well Sandra, I haven't had a chance to talk with him since his squadron went on a training flight to Rhine-Main, Germany. He should be back in a few more days. Since you're going with the Ferrarie boy, I'm sure your dad will agree, so go ahead and tell him yes. What about this dinner? Do you have something planned?"

"Either fried chicken or *jambon* (ham) and *fromage* (cheese) sandwiches. Fred hasn't given me his order yet but I'm guessing fried chicken though. Most of the girls want everybody to bring a different kind of cake so we can share 'cause Miss Glover said she could get the school to donate ice cream. Remember, I'm Sandy now not Sandra."

"Okay, dear. Sounds like a plan; we can buy everything at the commissary on Friday after school. Will you want potato salad or coleslaw to go with the chicken?"

"Potato salad; Miss Glover said the school will provide the potato chips and drinks, so I guess we're set. Thanks so much, Mom."

I called Linda to tell her the good news. "With mid-terms coming up after the hayride, can we start on some type of study plan? I know you can hardly think of anything but who asked you to the hayride, but I really need to start now so I won't have to cram."

Linda replied, "Yes, I know you are right, but this is my first real date with David. He tries to call me every night and my dad won't let me talk if my homework isn't done. I'm having a *problème.*" (problem)

"Could we plan for just an hour after we get home from school every day?"

"Neat. You could come over to my house one day, and I'll come to yours the next."

"Cool."

Saturday morning dawned sunny and bright with only a little chill in the *automne* (fall) air. Linda and I studied every afternoon, so we were ready for a break. We planned to fix our meal together and our parents had agreed to drive only one way so no one would have to drive to the post twice. I felt thrilled to have Linda's parents pick us up at the end of the hayride and be allowed to spend the night.

Everyone met at the junior high and loaded their *nourriture* (food), *couvertures* (blankets), guitars and bales of *foin* (hay). Steve started breaking down the bales with help from several other boys so everyone would have a comfortable place to sit on the flatbed *camion* (truck). As soon as everyone was loaded onto this different form of transportation, the driver drove to other side of the Army Post. The park was quite small, but there were many tall trees and it almost felt like a little forest as we drove through to the pond where a fire would be built while everyone ate dinner.

Linda, David, Fred and I jumped off the truck as soon as it stopped by the pond. We wanted to get the best seat by the large stack of split wood before dinner started. The ride over had been fun because some of the boys played songs on their guitars. Everyone gathered around the fire, now blazing brightly, and started to eat. When it was time to leave, each cleaned up their place and jumped up onto the truck to snuggle in the hay and sing along with the guitars.

At school on Monday, I sat with Linda in *une cercle des pupitres* (a circle of desks) with Janice and Margo and shared our lunches. The main topic was the recent hayride. Since Linda and I had dates, Janice and Margo were the only ones commenting on some of the outlandish behavior they saw.

"No one ever said or even suggested the purpose of this hayride was to see who could make-out the longest," Janice said sternly.

"Well, we were told dates weren't necessary, so I just came with Jill and Janice," Margo added, twisting her long black hair around her finger.

"You guys are starting to sound like my parents. There were plenty of *jeux* (games) and singing to keep busy and not look at us," Linda replied harshly, reaching up and back to tighten her red pony tail.

"I kinda agree with Linda," Sandy said. "I sure didn't know having a date meant a make-out session, even though I did have my very first kiss. Fred and I have been camping with our families ever since we moved here. His family is like an extension of mine and I guess to me, he's like an older brother. You know, his kiss was nice and all, but he can't ever be more than just a friend." My face scrunched up with concern, knowing this new information changed how I now thought about Fred.

"I'd have traded places with you in a minute if I'd have known," Margo said. "I've had a crush on him since we started going to Paris American High (PAHS). Several of the tenth grade girls couldn't believe he asked you, Sandy. But, now I can see why since you claim to have been friends for so long. You were a safe date."

"A safe date? What do you mean?" I asked hesitantly.

"No pressure to make out. You said he only kissed you once," Margo replied, continuing to twist her long black hair around her index finger.

"Yeah, so what? It's no big deal."

"That's just what I mean, no pressure. Didn't you see how Steve reacted when David kissed Linda? I mean we all know how un-cool Steve can be sometimes, but he's such fun especially when he starts playing his guitar. I've heard he's a great kisser. I'd like to be his date just once," Margo replied.

"Well, when Janice's *mère* (mom) called mine to tell her about all the kissing, my mom couldn't believe I didn't tell her," Margo said.

"What? You told on us Janice? No wonder we were in trouble," Linda answered with a frown.

"Leave her alone," I said. "Besides, I know Janice. I bet it was Jill who spilled her guts, right?"

Just then, Jill walked over. "I told all right. I was just a little upset 'cause I didn't get asked. My favorite hopeful asked someone else and I was really ticked." She frowned and blinked rapidly, her blue eyes showing disappointment.

"You guys, knock it off. We don't need to fight and ruin our friendship over some guy. Maybe we can be on the committee for the next one and resolve this stuff so our folks will let us go on the spring hayride," added Janice, always the peacemaker.

"Yeah guys, Janice's right. She always seems to figure out a way to solve problems when our parents threaten to never let us go out with guys again," I answered.

The *sonnette* (bell) rang and we scrambled to pick up our trash and get to our lockers before the tardy *sonnette* sounded. Only a few notes were passed during the afternoon classes to finish handling the hayride hoop-la.

By the end of the month, as the last leaves of fall continued to empty each branch on *les arbres* (trees) in town, the four of us met at the bakery in Bois-le-Roi for our final Saturday morning bike ride. The scrumptious smell of freshly baked bread and pastries encouraged us to run inside and pick out our weekly treat of brioche, petit baguette, or fruit tart.

Usually we would ride down to the Seine River and stop on *le pont* (the bridge). Then, we looked downstream toward Vic and Joanne's gigantic castle-like house. It faced the road in front of the famous river which flowed south from Paris. If she stood on the balcony, we could ride over. We had set up this signal when the idea popped into Joanne's head, always filled with ideas to get anyone to come see her. Her dad, a full colonel in the Army, didn't allow any phone privileges on the week-end since he was in charge of something on the Army Post none of the four of us ever understood.

"I must have an open phone line 24 hours a day" was the only explanation he ever gave to his children.

Like the others, she knew it was a useless argument. So weekend plans were always arranged before *vendredi* (Friday). Today however there was no one on the balcony, even though we waited an extra ten minutes.

"There goes my chance to see her gorgeous brother Vic," Margo lamented, rolling her dark brown eyes.

"Yeah, I think he knows you have a crush on him," Janice giggled. Her grey-green eyes brightened and widened at this thought.

"Well, what should we do instead?" I asked. "We have a full *heure* (hour) before we have to be home. I'm sure not going to be there one minute before my time is over."

For the first time all fall, Linda came up with an idea and all agreed. We crossed the bridge and rode down the other side of the river, north toward a campground. *Le jour* (the day) was sunny and a cool breeze blew over *l'eau (*the water). We knew the first snowfall would be coming soon and many months would pass before we'd be allowed our first ride of *le printemps* (the spring). On the way home, Margo mentioned, "This will probably be our last fall ride of ninth grade since next year we'll be going up to PAHS. I can hardly wait."

"Lucky you," I lamented. "Remember me 'cause my dad's tour ends in *juin* (June) and we'll be going home."

"Tough news. You will really miss something extra special, getting to live in Paris" Margo replied. "I just can't wait to be away from home and have those neat make-out bus rides up to Paris."

"What do you mean? I haven't heard about this," I asked. "How cool for those who are dating. . ."

"Depends on who you talk to," Linda interrupted. "Jill says sometimes the noises from kissing gets to be embarrassing for those who aren't with someone and are just trying *coucher to (sleep)*, *étudier (to study)*, or even *parle* (talk)."

"Well just give me a chance to try," Margo said as she twisted a strand of black hair around her finger. "I have all summer to find a boyfriend so I'll have someone to enjoy the long bus ride with instead of being *toute seul.* " (all alone)

In December, I was the unfortunate one to have to miss the Christmas dance. My family had planned a vacation to Spain during the long holiday break and we were leaving a week before the vacation started.

"All the decorations we are making are really going to make that old Quonset hut look beautiful," Linda told me over the phone the night before my family left on vacation. "I'll tell you anything and everything when you get back, so have a great trip, take lots of pictures and don't forget to send me *une carte postale* (a post card).

« *Joyeux Noel and Bonne année.* » (Merry Christmas and Happy New Year)

The holiday vacation was really enjoyable for our family as we saw so many fantastic historical sights, such as the famous Prado art museum in Madrid and the Sagrada Familia church started by Gaudi in 1883 and still not finished. A famous architect, he worked on this building until he died in 1926. For all the interesting things we saw my head and heart were back at the dance. On the drive home, I finished my book sooner than planned and then became anxious to finish the trip so I could hear about all the fun I missed at the dance.

As soon as we drove into the backyard, I jumped out of the Volkswagen bus to be the first to use the phone.

"Not so fast, young lady," my dad called out. "Get back here and help unload some of this luggage."

As soon as I finished, I asked my mom if I could use the phone to call Linda. But, she reminded me I'd have to wait until my father had checked for messages. I ran up the two flights of stairs to unpack and spread out the gifts I brought back for my friends.

Mom stood at the bottom of the staircase as she called up to the third floor a few minutes later.

"Children, come downstairs, quickly."

"What's wrong Mom?" Harvey asked.

"Please get your sisters and come down immediately," mom answered.

As we came into the living room, dad sat in his recliner chair with *une sourire* (a smile) on his face, an unusual sight to see. He told us to sit down because he had some good news to share.

"I've just found out my extension was accepted. We'll be able to stay in France for an additional year." He motioned for my brother to come closer to him as he said, "Harvey, I know you've been unhappy this year at your boarding school, so I decided you will return to the junior high next year to start ninth grade and begin preparing for our return to the states."

Carole Anne and I looked over at our brother with smiles on our faces. We knew what a tough year he'd had as a boarder in the all boy school. He had not liked staying there overnight at all. We were thrilled to see an expression of gratitude and relief on his face.

"You really mean it, Dad? Oh, thanks so much. I'll work really hard to finish up this year and improve my French. I can't wait to go to junior high and speak English all day!"

"Dad, does this mean I'll be able to go to high school in Paris?"

With a stern look on his face and not even a tiny smile, he answered "Yes, young lady. As long as you keep your grades up this year, I don't see a problem with you living in the dorm," he replied.

I could hardly contain my joy. I asked as politely as possible, "Dad, are you finished with all your messages? I'd like to call Linda and tell her the good news."

"Sure Sandra. I'm finished. Don't be long though, I have a few calls to make to the states." He then looked at my mom and grinned.

I could hardly get to the phone fast enough. While I waited for the operator to put the call through, my knees started to shake.

"Hi, Jill, can I speak to Linda? Hi there, yes, we're back; I want to hear about the dance, but wait just a minute. You won't believe the fantastic news I just heard. We get to stay another year! My dad put in for an extension and it has been accepted. Isn't this the best New Year's present ever?"

"Cool. I'm so glad we'll both get to go to PAHS. Will you be my roommate?"

« Mais oui ! » (But of course, yes)

II. THE OTHER MOM

Everyone is sure having fun. Look at them: kicking, laughing, running . . . I'm just standing here all alone at the other end of the field. This is no fun. My mom and dad said I would like playing soccer with my friends. I'm just standing here in front of this net, doing NOTHING thought second grader, Allison Brown.

As Mrs. Brown watched her eight year old daughter stretch her short arms overhead, she saw her grimace as she continually kicks at the dirt. She commented to her husband, "Allison looks frustrated. Guess she's not enjoying herself today."

Allison thought to herself: *Maybe I will leave. I'll just walk over to my mom and tell her I don't want to play anymore I bet no one will even notice.*

Dr. Brown looked toward his daughter after his wife commented on her attitude. He saw Allison make a face and kick a few dirt clumps out of her way as she took one look at her teammates gathered around the slowly moving ball in the middle of the soccer field. She marched defiantly off the field. The referee blew her whistle.

This is much better, Allison decided. *I'll just stand here and watch them play and explain to mom and dad why I don't want to do this* anymore.

Fourteen year old Bethany Montgomery, the referee,

approached Allison saying, "You can't just walk off the field in the middle of a game. Are you feeling sick?" She motioned for her to go back onto the field.

Great, Allison thought while standing there with her arms folded. *Now my coach is talking to my parents and the ref. What's the big deal? This is only a boring game.*

As Bethany blew the whistle again, everyone left the field and ran over to Mrs. Brown, the parent in charge of refreshments today, who provided the orange slices and glasses of water. *On no,* Allison thought. *Now the coach is calling me and my parents over to where he is standing. Guess I won't have time for any snack.*

Coach Reed spoke carefully, trying not to show too much emotion. "Allison, what's wrong? Don't you remember how important the goalie position is to a team?"

"Coach, this is sooo boring. I'm not having any fun like the rest of the team. The ball never comes to me and I'm not getting a chance to kick for a goal."

As her coach bent down on both knees he looked concerned and said to her, "Do you remember when we spoke about the rules of the game? I reminded each player what their job was on the field and what each is to do when the ref or I blow the whistle."

"Yes, I remember." She looked worried, with no smile on her cute freckled face. "I don't like standing in front of the net all the time. Nothing ever happens there. I don't want to play anymore." She brushed her black bangs off her creased forehead.

"All right Allison. You will stand on the sidelines for the

rest of the game."

While watching everyone else play, she remembered when her twin brother Alan said soccer is fun. *Sure, he is the one running all the time and kicking the ball while I have to just stand at the net. Maybe the new kid they pick will like playing goalie and then I could run and play. Maybe I could just have my friends come to my house and play in our back yard. We could just run all around and have no whistles to stop us.*

The drive home from the game seemed too long today. Allison realized how tired she felt just sitting with the seatbelt on. As her head drifted over to her brother's shoulder, she dozed until they reached home.

"Alli, would you come over here please. We need to talk," said her mother. Allison knew what was coming when she heard the nickname she didn't like.

"Can't I change out of my uniform first, Mom? Does Alan have to come too?" Tears started to form in her brown eyes as she tugged as her black pigtails and pulled the red ribbons off. *Oh well, I might as well get this over with so I can go upstairs and change.*

Looking from her mom to her dad, Allison knew she didn't want to hear what would be coming. She sat down on the sofa and waited.

"We paid a lot of money for you and Alan to be on this team; then we bought you a new uniform and shoes. Quitters are not part of the Brown family," her mom spoke sternly, shaking her freckled face from side to side.

Her father continued. "You must finish what you started or this could be a pattern for your whole life if you think you can quit anytime things don't go your way."

Great. I can see I'm not getting any support, even from mom.

Her dad continued. "Alli, you can't quit just because you don't like the position you are playing. How about this idea? I'll clear my schedule every afternoon for an hour and practice with you and your brother." He looked at her for a positive response. "Do you ask questions when Coach Reed explains things you don't understand?"

"Well, I guess I could practice a little more. I do like playing outside and kicking the ball is fun, Daddy," she answered.

Then she quickly remembered a continuing thought which had been bothering her for a long time: *when my other mom did not want to do something, she did not have to and no one tried to change her mind. Maybe I should tell this to mom and she'll understand.*

As she started to walk out of the room, she yelled to her brother, "Hey Alan, do you want to play goalie next week? I'll let you play with my Nintendo game any time you want for a whole week." She turned back to her mom and asked, "Mom, could I ask Coach Reed if he will give some of the others time to play goalie? They will know the feeling of having the ball kicked at you and there is nothing you can do to stop it from going over the line."

"Sure, good idea dear." Mrs. Brown answered, smiling at her daughter.

As she walked up the stairs, Allison decided she would talk to her mom about her other mom problem later.

She started thinking about a solution to her playing goalie. *If I went to school everyday, I could talk to some of the other girls and ask them to take turns playing goalie. Maybe home schooling wasn't such a good idea 'cause I don't get to see my friends very much.* Her friend Stephanie told her their teacher would tell them when they had to change subjects and sometimes when the students weren't finished with what they were working on, some teachers would get mad.

Allison remembered her mom saying how long they had waited for children and they were so happy when they were able to adopt. She thought learning would be so much more fun if she and Alan stayed home for schooling. *Mom keeps saying she doesn't want to let us go. Does this have anything to do with why we drive such a long way into the city every month to see our other mom?*

While sprawled on her comfortable twin bed, she pondered, again: *sometimes I get what adoption means and sometimes I don't.* She remembered when her parents explained adoption to her and Alan. When they would go to her dad's office sometimes (where he worked as an obstetrician) and see all the ladies sitting there with big tummies, Dr. Brown would explain babies grow inside of a lady before they are born. Some ladies can't grow a baby inside them, so they adopt one. Every time she and Alan would go to the store, they would adopt a toy.

Allison sat up and looked out the window as her thoughts shifted to her other mom. *Whenever we see her, she looks just like me and Alan 'cause her hair is black and straight and her eyes are brown, just like ours. Grandmother O'Leary, mom's mom, says this lady has an Italian background, like my dad.* Then she remembered seeing pictures of her mom from Grandmother O'Leary's scrapbook. Her mom has blue eyes, freckles and reddish brown hair. She looked more like Grandmother O'Leary as a young woman, from Ireland.

A sad look came over Allison's face as she thought about her other mom. *Maria is nice, but she doesn't take care of us.* She looked out the window at the leaves starting to change colors. She really wanted to know more about her other mom and why she didn't keep her and Alan.

None of my friends have two moms. When I talk to them about my other mom, they seem mixed up too. My mom wants me to call Maria birth-mom so I understand the difference between my two moms. Allison felt like yelling out loud, *I can sure know the difference from a mother who cares for me everyday and one I only visit once a month.*

Sure enough, her dad kept his promise and came home every afternoon to practice the goal keeper position with them. Getting this extra help made playing more fun, especially when Coach Reed let others take turns to play goalie.

The next Friday night, they were called downstairs just before going to bed to find out a babysitter would be coming over.

"What happened to Grandmother O'Leary?"

"She is playing bridge tonight with some friends, so we asked our neighbor if she could recommend anyone. She told us Bethany Montgomery is very reliable," his mom said.

"Oh yeah, she refereed our game," Allison mentioned.

"Here she is now," said her dad as they heard a car door

close. She walked inside, her blue eyes sparkling with recognition.

After their parents left, Alan whispered, "I guess we could play some games with her so we won't have to go to bed."

Bethany said, "How's soccer practice coming along? I heard your dad was taking some extra time to help you improve."

"So far, so good," Allison replied.

"Can I read you a story before bedtime?"

Alan answered, "Can't we play a game instead?"

"Sorry, bedtime. Your mom said we have time for only one story." Alan shrugged his shoulders and left quietly. He said he'd play in his room.

When Allison picked out her favorite book, <u>Are you adopted too?</u> Bethany said, "Oh, this is one of my favorite stories. My sister Brittany and I are adopted," she continued, "and my mom used to read this to us when we were little. A couple of my friends are adopted too. We have often talked about how well adoption is explained to children in this book."

I can't believe this, Allison thought. *Maybe Bethany can explain this adoption stuff and having two moms. I wonder if I should call Alan. Just because we are twins doesn't mean we have to share everything though . . . maybe I should talk to her first.*

"Bethany, I have two moms and sometimes I just don't get how this works. My birth-mom lives in the city and we see her once a month. Alan says since she doesn't take care of us and we only talk for a little while, what's the big deal about going to visit her?" She stopped for a minute and looked closely at Bethany. "Do you know who your other mom is and have you met her? Do you look like her? Do you miss her and do you see her ever?"

"Wait a minute, Allison," Bethany said. "You are asking so many questions; one at a time, please. My sister and I lived with our real parents until we came here, about seven years ago. My dad and mom didn't get along and they fought a lot. Many nights there wasn't any dinner because they used their money to buy liquor. Anyway, one day a lady came to the door and took us away. Later my new mom and dad told me our parents just couldn't care for us anymore, and the state welfare office made the decision to come in and take us away so we could be adopted into a more stable family."

"Wow, I just can't believe this . . . you lived with your real parents. Sometimes I wish I could too, but I don't know anything about my real father."

Bethany looked at her with a very serious face. "Allison, you are so lucky to have someone who wants you and loves you. Just because someone is your birth parent doesn't mean they will love and take care of you . . ."

Allison interrupted, "Yeah, like taking me to soccer practice and making me play as a goal keeper."

Bethany nodded. "Yes, doing things you don't want to do is part of life. We all have choices to make everyday. I don't even know if I want to be a parent because I want to be a vet and care for animals. Going to vet school after college will take a lot of time and money and I'm not sure I could do both. I know I'm only 14, but raising a child is very hard work."

"But I look so much like my other mom, Bethany, even though I really don't know her or love her like my mom. I mean, she seems nice, but I'm happy here."

"Who takes care of you everyday?" Bethany asked. "Who fixes your meals, reads stories and hugs you when you feel sad? I know some of this is hard to understand at your age, but as you grow older and keep asking questions, you'll figure everything out." She reached over to give her a big hug.

"To live with people who fight all the time is terrible. They never feel good because they drink too much and you rarely get hugs or good food to eat. Brittany and I love our new parents and we have lots to compare. We see the love they have for each other every single day. Sometimes, only for a few seconds, I wish we could have stayed together but our parents didn't know how to stop drinking, help us with our school work or spend time with us without fighting."

She looked out the window and sighed. "We weren't happy there and we never had any fun. We sure never talked about the things my new parents share with us." She reached over to hold Allison's hand and give it a little squeeze.

"To raise children to grow up to become responsible adults is really a hard job and a lot more important than some people think."

Allison started to cry just a little because she felt sad when Bethany was trying to explain this parent stuff. She wanted to be like the other children. "What do you think about seeing my other mom?"

Bethany hesitated. "Look, you have to decide for yourself how you really feel about Maria. If this is confusing for you, tell your mom how you feel. Does Alan agree?"

Allison stopped sniffling and thought about some of the conversations when she and Alan had argued about which mom they should really live with forever.

"He thinks we have a great life and I shouldn't mess anything up. I do love my parents and only once in a while I wonder about living with her and what my days would be like in the city." She walked over to her dresser to pick up a tissue, wipe her eyes and blow her nose. Bethany gave her some new ideas to think about adoption.

"My mom says someone who really cares about her babies and what kind of life they will have is a very considerate lady. When she can't care for her babies, she wants to do the right thing. This is really a very hard choice. Finally, after thinking about what is really best for her babies, she knows she needs to give them to someone else who can raise them right."

Allison wiped her nose and smiled a little at Bethany. "Alan and I have fun with our parents and I like when we are together. I can see they do care about us. This was the only way they could get any babies. So . . . I guess right now, I want to be like other girls and have only one mom."

Bethany didn't want to make this any more difficult. She could see by the long rambling sentences Allison spoke, she felt troubled about her choices. She decided to talk with her mom and Mrs. Brown about the best way to handle this problem. Remembering when she and Brittany were going through this same confusion, she felt a closeness to this confused little girl, and really wanted to help.

"I'll tell you what Allison, let's read this great story now and we can talk more later. You look tired. We have brought up lots of things tonight." She opened the book to the first page, then said. "Besides, I play soccer too and I really like seeing younger girls out on the playing field. Your coach says maybe some day we can have a travel team just for girls. If you continue playing, you will improve. By the time you are in high school there could be a girl's team and you could earn a varsity letter."

Later, as she snuggled under her pastel pink polka dot sheet and matching blanket, Allison thought maybe things would work out after all. *I do want to keep the parents I have and only have one mom,* she decided. *I'll just tell them I will work hard at learning how to play soccer because I would have more fun playing with only girls.*

Bethany seemed to have just drifted off to sleep when she heard car doors close and the kitchen door open. Her streaked red bangs hung over her eyebrows as she woke up and she pushed them off her forehead. During those few quiet moments, she decided she'd better tell them what happened.

"Dr. and Mrs. Brown, I hope you won't mind, well, Allison talked to me about her other mom, I mean Maria so I told her about my birth-parents."

"What?" they both said at once. Dr. Brown ran his short stubby fingers through his graying black hair.

Then, as she proceeded to tell them about her confusion with having two mothers, she said slowly, "I told her what happened to us and I think she doesn't want to see Maria anymore."

Dr. Brown's black eyebrows rose on his creased forehead as his dark brown eyes became very somber. He lowered himself slowly onto the straight-backed kitchen chair and put his head in his hands, elbows on the table.

"I was afraid of this Vanessa. Maybe we shouldn't have told the children this young, and," he hesitated, "bringing Maria into the picture. . ." He didn't finish his thought as he looked into his wife's troubled face, eyebrows wrinkled with concern.

Vanessa Brown appeared somewhat miffed as she looked at Bethany who was standing helplessly beside the wooden kitchen table, cluttered with piles of mail and medical folders. She wondered if she had made a mistake asking Bethany to come tonight. Quickly, she questioned herself: *What if they had not told the children? Could this have been a big mistake?* Mrs. Brown didn't realize what was really bothering Allison last week. Yet, when her daughter walked off the soccer field during the game, so defiantly, Vanessa realized she should have known there was something on her mind.

As her perfectly polished pink fingernails tapped on the table, Mrs. Brown said: "Bethany, I'm not sure this was a good idea. When I found out about your family from Mrs. Nelson, I hoped maybe you might be the one who could alleviate some of Allison's questions. I had no idea she felt this way about Maria. I think adopted children should know who their birth mother is in order to prepare them for understanding adoption. Now I am questioning my own motives. What did Alan say?" Bethany told them about the rest of the evening's conversation.

While her husband drove Bethany home, Vanessa decided to soak in the whirlpool tub. As she felt the soothing bubbles all around her tired body, her two childhood friends, Emily and Amanda came to mind. She had never forgotten their shocked faces when they had stumbled onto a sordid secret, hardly talked about in those days. They had been quite devastated when by accident, they learned of their adoptions.

Of course, I could never have known I would not be able to have children of my own and I would some day adopt. Wasn't this the best decision for them? She lamented, *no one ever said children would come with instructions. What was I thinking? Emily and Amanda were so confused with the upsetting information; they couldn't believe their parents weren't their real parents.* Her thoughts jumbled together and she continued to remember their terrified looks as they told her of the secret they stumbled onto, much to their dismay. Neither set of parents had told their daughters they were adopted.

As her husband walked into the bedroom about fifteen minutes later, Vanessa called out from the bathroom, "Dear, maybe we should reconsider our monthly meetings with Maria. Can we talk about this tonight?"

Dr. Brown stared into the bathroom at his wife who looked confused, even though she had relaxing bubbles swirling all around her. Not knowing what to say, he responded, "Not tonight," as he undressed slowly and climbed into their worn heirloom oak bed without his cleansing evening shower. He pulled the wrinkled sheet and lightweight blue and yellow patchwork quilt over his weary face and remembered all the years of trying to conceive a child. After many tests, they found out they couldn't have their own. Then came not one baby, but twins. Both were available for adoption. Everything they had prayed for finally came true: they were a family.

"I have late rounds at the hospital," he lamented, his voice sounded a little shaky. "What about Maria? I have a vague memory," He stopped in mid-sentence, sat up and looked into the bathroom. "Did she really want these visits? Whose idea was this anyway, Vanessa, mine or yours?" He looked more intently at his wife, his forehead continually creased with thought.

"Could we just send pictures? We'll have to continue this discussion when I get home from work. Maybe you are right; we need to reconsider these monthly meetings." He fell back onto the worn mattress and snuggled under the blue and yellow striped sheets, his brain overloaded with confusing thoughts. *Lord, what should we do?* He changed his nightly prayers and asked for guidance for this decision.

The next morning bright sunshine filtered through fluttering yellow chintz curtains in the master bedroom. Chirping birds in the large oak tree and a gentle breeze coming in through the open windows helped the Brown family wake up. A solution would have to be reached soon. Together they would decide what direction their family would take as they continued to walk down this un-chartered path of their life.

They both knew there will be only one mom.

III. A HAUNTED HOUSE

"What scares you? I really want to know," Jeff Jones asked his sixteen year old daughter in preparation for deciding what trick to play on her for Halloween.

Now as Melissa drove diligently in the relentless rain, the first sharp curve of state road 39 came upon her too quickly. Part of Pineview Reservoir came into view. Her parent's mid-sized car skidded from one side of the road to the other while she tried to maintain control. As she continued to move forward ever so slowly, the rain and wind began to decrease and a heavy fog seemed to come out of nowhere and swallow up the road. She had only driven this road around the reservoir twice before, in the daylight. She felt a little scared right now, wishing her driving classes had been longer and at least one had been after dark.

She never saw the next turn and her car skidded off the road into a small ditch, already overflowing with water from the non-stop rain. She looked out the window and saw a glimmer of light in the distance. She decided she'd better get out of the car as quickly as possible and run toward the light. Her palms continued to sweat as she tried to open the door. There was no movement. *"I'm scared now, dad."* She remembered the question he had asked her last night.

Suddenly she remembered the sun roof and pushed the switch. Slowly the top of the car opened. Melissa climbed out as quickly as possible. The raging rainstorm almost blew her off the car. She tried to get down and away from the swirling water in the ditch. She jumped from the hood of the car over the water and slid down an embankment, grabbing a tree limb just in time to climb onto a sagging stump.

Melissa managed to slide off the sagging stump and get a firm hold on the wet ground. She knew if she could just get to the light she'd be able to use a phone and call home. She didn't have a jacket or umbrella and the pelting rain made the walking treacherous. *I can do this,* she thought to herself as she put one foot in front of the other while trying to keep her balance as she climbed carefully up the slippery slope. The existing embankment was steeper than she realized. *Oh no, I left my purse in the car. At least if someone finds my car they'll be able to report the accident and maybe call my parents,* she decided.

So many terrifying thoughts floated through her head, she had to keep telling herself to focus on her goal: the light in the distance. As she trudged over the saturated ground, she wondered why she wasn't getting any closer to the light. Not only was she getting more tired, but she felt soaked to the skin and a chill crept down her back. *Keep on walking, one step at a time,* she said to herself.

Earlier the same night, three weary teens struggled down from Flat Mountain, still covered in a blanket of white powder. Their snow shoes strained over the heavily packed snow. They had become separated from their church group while hiking in the back country of Powder Mountain. The darkness encouraged them to find warmth and water. What they really wanted was a glowing fire and something warm to drink. Then they would be able to call home, saying they were alright. A glimmer of light in the distance seemed to be the perfect goal.

As they approached this light, patches of faded paint barely covered the worn clapboard house which stood in the middle of a five acre parcel, along with only a few ragged tree stumps for neighbors. Most of the windows were broken and a few had cracks in the panes. The wooden porch sagged on the left side and the stair planks were broken into odd shaped pieces. Three of the four columns were still holding up a roof overhang which barely covered the rotting porch. The top screen on the storm door had a jagged rip down the right side and the metal handle had a missing screw to hold the bracket in place. The main door had deep indentations in the middle and the bottom had big scratches on the left as though an animal tried to get inside.

"Look at the smoke coming from the chimney. Do you think someone really lives there?" Sixteen year old Richard yelled back to his friends.

"As long as we can use the phone and get water, I don't care how bad the place looks," Jason yelled back. At eighteen, he was the oldest of the students.

Chris, at seventeen, appeared to be the most pensive of the group. He seemed to be the only one concerned as he looked closely at what seemed to be a dead house.

"How can there be smoke coming from a chimney when this place looks deserted? I think I'll wait here until you guys go inside first and see what you find."

The boys arrived at the dilapidated house and cautiously listened for any signs of life. They heard nothing and hesitated briefly before opening what was left of the storm door, hanging on the flimsy frame by only a large rusted bolt. Each looked hesitantly past the door.

"Well, what are you waiting for Jason? Go inside."

"Doesn't this place seem a little creepy to you? Really looks empty," Chris commented as he took off his soaked gloves and ran cold callused hands through his short black hair, shaking off the wet drops as he turned his head upside down.

"You go in first, Richard and we'll follow on your tail," Jason said as he too took off his soaked gloves. At six feet tall, with the most 'gorgeous' strawberry blond hair, according to all the girls at Christian Heritage High School, Jason worried about his friends during this long cold night.

All three walked cautiously inside the front room, together as though one. This first room had no furniture inside and cobwebs hung from each corner. They stopped and didn't move, waiting for something or someone to jump out. Then they proceeded into the next room where to their surprise a small fire, almost out, still burned. A stack of large cut pieces of wood had been stacked next to what was left of a fireplace. Three mugs of cold hot chocolate sat on a broken mantel.

"What's going on, some kind of joke?" Chris asked as he started to wring out the excess water from his soaking wet ski cap. "How'd this get here?"

"Well, right this second I really don't care, I just want to taste something hot," Richard replied. His dark auburn hair felt really wet and he bent over to shake out the excessive water.

"Yeah, but wait guys; this stuff could be really bad. It is definitely not hot. Don't you think this is kinda weird, almost as though someone is setting a trap for us; no one lives here yet who put these mugs and wood here?" Jason asked.

"Hold on a second; let's not hurry." Chris took off his soaked ski jacket and stood with his back to the non existent fire, wishing for instant warmth. He put two more logs on and bent down to blow a little air onto the coals to start the fire again. In a few minutes, they felt the instant warmth of these flames.

"Right now I really don't care. Just let me have a sip. We can think later," Richard answered as he took off his gloves, jacket and hat and ran his cold hand though his short formerly spiked hair, now sticky from hair gel.

All three sat down, each looking in a different direction as if waiting for someone to jump out and yell, "Surprise, you're on Candid Camera!"

Minutes seem to tick away slowly as the boys held onto the cold cups. A strange sound perked up their attention as though someone or something splashed in the puddles outside. With each splash, they looked at each other wide-eyed. All three stood up quickly and peered around a cracked wall toward the broken screen door, shivering with fright. They heard a squeak and steps coming from next room. They started to huddle together quickly looking desperately for some object to use as protection.

Melissa was stunned to see the three frightened faces staring at her as she walked ever so slowly into the room. She collapsed onto the floor without speaking.

All three ran toward her as she fell, trying to catch her before she hit the floor. Richard caught her head in his hands as the rest of her body hit the floor with a thud. Chris and Jason helped maneuver her near the fire. Richard rubbed her hands to give her some instant warmth.

Several minutes later, Melissa woke up to see three concerned faces looking at her with relief. She sat up and faced the fire, trying to get warm. Her body shivered under her soaking wet clothes. Her short red streaked brown hair clung to her face and neck. Her freckled face, wet with rain drops was quickly wiped off with the back of her hand. Her green pensive eyes, full of questions looked at each of them.

"Where am I and who are you?" she asked as she introduced herself, pushing her soaked hair away from her eyes, still wide open with surprise.

As Richard introduced everyone, he replied, "We're not sure exactly where we are. We hiked down from Powder Mountain after we became separated from our hiking group. We saw a light and found this place, with what was left of a fire going and cups of hot chocolate. But then the light disappeared just as we arrived."

"This is way too weird, but we don't want to go back out in this rain. We are just too tired and wet."

"You are really lucky you made the hike down without any trouble. I ran off the road into a ditch and walked toward a light which sure isn't here now." She tried to wring out her wet hair. "Guess we'll just have to stay here tonight and in the morning get our bearings. I'm sure not going back out into this mess. Tomorrow we can walk back to the road to find a phone."

She looked from one concerned face to another while momentarily trying to guess how the wood and chocolate could have found it's way here.

"Oh no, my watch is broken, so I don't even know the time. Listen guys, I sure can't figure out how a fire was going either, but scary or not, we have to stay here tonight." She shivered. "Are any of you going back out into this mess? I'm really cold and need to get warm, dry my clothes and get some sleep."

"There is no way I'm going back out tonight." said Jason.

"Sleep? There's no way I'm going to close one eye in this place. Something weird is going on and I'm not taking any chances for whoever is waiting for us to get me when I'm sleeping," Chris added. "You guys can sleep if you want to, but I'm staying awake. Melissa, none of us has a watch either."

Jason looked to Chris and agreed. "I'll stay awake with you. I don't know what's going on here either, but let's pray for safety. The rest of you can sleep if you can and we will keep watch."

Somehow they managed to get through what was left of the night, with Jason and Chris dozing part of the time. Luckily for them, no one showed up and they kept the fire going with the stack of wood.

The morning came with a bright sun filtering in through broken window panes. Jason was the first one to rush out.

As he stepped off the sagging porch he tripped over the broken stairs, fell and twisted his ankle. To the right he saw a huge light on a stand of some type. He stood up and limped to the steps as everyone else was coming out.

"Jason, are you limping? What happened to your ankle?"

"I fell off the porch; but it's no big deal. But look here. What do you make of this large light on a stand, facing the side of what's left of this house?"

Melissa looked at each of them. "Look I don't know what this is either, but I have a proposal for you to consider before we leave. In Minnesota where I'm from, there are cabins out in the woods and people always replenish what they use for the next person. We were saved because someone did this, so I think we should at least replenish the wood for the next person who shows up, lost, and cold."

"I don't mind filling up the fireplace with wood," Richard said, "but we had good sized logs which were cut. There's nothing around here but scraps of wood."

"Since there's no water, we can't really clean the cups, so let's just rinse them out with some of this standing water, Melissa said. "Jason, can you walk?"

"I'm fine. I'll limp along and see how my ankle feels. I just want to get to a phone. I'm sure people spent the night looking for us and I want my folks to know I'm alright. Since we survived the night

and storm without this place falling down around us, I guess prayers
do help."

"All right then, let's pick up as much of this scrap wood as we
can find and get going."

Lost in their own thoughts, the group started walking toward
the rising sun which was actually in the opposite direction from the
road. Even though they were in a hurry, the pace was slow enough for
Jason to limp along. After what seemed forever, they came upon a
barn inside a fenced pasture.

"Can anyone see if there is a gate?" Melissa asked. "I'm not
anxious to climb over this metal fence unless absolutely necessary."

"I'll go around to the side," Richard said as he ran to the
corner of the fenced off area. Sure enough, about 500 feet away was a
gate. He yelled back to them, "Take your time. I'm going to the
house."

He knocked on the door of the white clapboard house and
figured someone would be up since this looked like a working farm.
Suddenly, his nostrils picked up a smell of bacon. He hoped he would
be able to eat soon. He ate his last meal at lunch, before they started
their hike yesterday afternoon. *Must be someone's breakfast,* he
thought. The door opened and Richard blurted out: "Can you help us?
We've been lost from our group hiking on Powder Mountain since last
night and need a phone."

An older woman took wire rimmed glasses off her head, put
them on and looked at him with surprise. "Son, do you know what
time it is? I've only just awakened and besides, there's no phone

service out here since the storm took out the electricity. We only have a rotary dial phone." She wore a plaid apron over her red flannel nightgown and her long graying hair had been tied with a red ribbon.

"No, I don't. What time is it? Can someone take us to a phone?"

"It's just a little before seven. Come on in and I'll see if my husband can take you. He's out in the pasture, feeding the cows and won't be back for at least another 10 minutes. I have no way to get in touch with him until he finishes."

By this time the rest of the group staggered up to the farm house and asked politely if they could come in, use the toilet and get something to drink. After introductions were made, Mrs. Becky Mancuso asked them if they'd like some hot chocolate.

"I ran off the road last night during the storm and walked toward a light in the middle of nowhere. Do you know anything about an old shack back behind your property?"

"There are several back there. Which way did you come?"

"We really don't know; we just walked toward the rising sun," Jason answered.

Mrs. Mancuso said, "Look, I'm sure you are hungry, so let me fix you some breakfast. I was just starting to cook bacon. My husband Joe is known for his sourdough pancakes down at the Sweets Store. He's out in the pasture so you might as well relax and eat something." She put more wood in a wood burning stove and put another pan on top to start frying eggs.

The Night Before

"Hey Jordan, did you turn off the light switch before you left the property?" Ty looked at him with concern.

"Can't remember if I did, but the timer was set. I'm not sure if Vicki told the second camera crew we'd be coming in around eight. She might have changed the second turn on/off switch" He pushed his Jazz basketball hat back onto his red streaked black hair.

Mike and Ty were two assistant co-producers of a film crew on location in Ogden Valley and had finished setting up the location for the first night's shooting, a scene on a deserted patch of farmland. Jordan, the director, had helped find this piece of land.

"Whoever scouted this valley and found the vacant farmhouse picked the perfect site," Mike mentioned as he drove carefully around the curves on state highway 39 toward Huntsville, the largest of the three towns in Ogden Valley. A terrible thunderstorm was just letting up and the wet road was seemed somewhat slippery. He turned onto a road leading into the small town located near the reservoir. The concierge at the Red Moose Lodge in Eden, one of the tri-towns, had recommended a local bar, the Shooting Star, for their first dinner. "They serve the best burgers around," he told anyone who'd asked. Those who lived in the valley knew the colorful place as the oldest continuous running bar in Utah. No one in the crew wanted to drive down the canyon road full of twists and turns back into Ogden on this first day of shooting, so they planned to meet here for dinner.

After they finished their delicious juicy hand made burgers, the rain continued to fall and they decided to go back to the motel knowing the light at the old farmhouse was on a timer. They posted a note saying tonight's shoot was canceled due to the weather.

The next morning everyone met at the Sweets Store for breakfast, ready to order the recommendation of their concierge, sourdough pancakes. They decided to start the night's shooting just after the sun went down since another rain storm had been scheduled to hit about nine.

"Vicki, will you go out this afternoon with your crew and get everything set for tonight? We can meet for dinner at six thirty up at Wolf Creek Restaurant," Ty said.

Everyone showed up promptly for dinner. Vicki and her crew were anxiously waiting for them at the bar.

She took off her Olympics jacket from the 2002 winter games in Salt Lake City, and ran manicured fingernails with red nail polish through her short streaked blond hair.

"There's a little problem at the place."

"What do you mean?" Jordan asked, putting on his dark rimed glasses.

"The fire place has a fresh pile of scrap wood ready for a fire, not the same wood we left last night, you know, those large split pieces we carried up there. The cups were empty, rinsed out and turned upside down on the mantel."

"No way; wonder what could have happened? Maybe the real owner, the ghost we were told lived there, came back," Mike said with a broad grin.

Vicki stated sternly, "Well I'm telling you, "I'm not going back there without the whole crew tonight." She looked at each one of them stating as positively as she could, "This shack is definitely a haunted house."

IV. ANOTHER LIFE

Mary Margaret and Elizabeth looked at the scene before them as if they were watching a scary play on the makeshift stage from their old one room schoolhouse near St. Louis. They were in shock as they stared wide-eyed looking around the circle of wagons which held their families. Their two brothers, parents, aunts, uncles and cousins were scattered on the ground like the pick-up-sticks game they used to play back home when their chores were finished. A group of Indians with painted faces stood in front of the sisters. Their conversation and arm gestures were threatening. The girls were grabbed from their hiding place behind a large wheel spoke and swung up onto sweating horses.

Days of riding bareback with the warriors brought them to a remote village in a small valley surrounded by massive mountains covered with evergreen trees. Remembering the excitement at the beginning of their trip out west, the girls had viewed in amazement the dark red dirt scattered with ragged rocks of all shapes and sizes. Small rolling hills in front of the mountains were covered with a variety of vegetation they had never seen before, showing beautiful shades of red, gold, brown and orange.

Mary Margaret remembered briefly her treasured spot in their wagon where she could look out from the peephole toward the north. She had also noticed the difference in lots of fluffy white clouds which were scattered randomly everywhere in the bright blue sky. These clouds had reminded her of their oversized family bed with the soft blue and white quilt where she used to nap. Instead of napping peacefully, she felt every bump on the trail.

Her uncle, Mark Martin, encouraged his brothers and their families to go on this trip by claiming, *"We're going to be a heading west . . . we'll git all the land we need fer farmin.'"*

Now the sisters had no idea where they were, as the days of traveling seemed to melt together. So many arduous hours of riding could have been seen as one continuous sight seeing trip for some adventurous types. The peaceful forests were beautiful in their silence. Within the wagon train group everyone felt in awe of the 'real west' as none of them had traveled outside St. Louis. Each day showed them new sights to enjoy on this flat prairie as they moved closer to the gigantic mountains.

Now, when they came into the village, many Indians had come up to welcome the warriors. Men and women were standing together, a very large group of different sizes and shapes. Most of the children talked rapidly as they pointed at the sisters. A weathered older man with a long white braid down his bare back limped toward them. He wore tan deerskin pants and beaded moccasins. He looked at them with a face full of questions as he touched Mary Margaret's red hair and freckles, and Elizabeth's light brown braids and patchwork dress. Both girls were shaking so badly they did not react to his massive wrinkled hands which touched them cautiously.

"Elizabeth, I'm really scared. What's going to happen to us now?"

A hand seemed to come out from nowhere, striking Mary Margaret across her mouth, silencing her immediately as tears ran down her freckled face. Elizabeth looked over toward Maggie, her sister's nickname, with an expression of fear. At fifteen, she wanted to be strong and comforting to her twelve year old sister. As she quickly put her arms around Maggie, an older woman in a beaded deerskin dress stepped forward to separate them. She frowned at both of them as Elizabeth was pulled away and pushed toward the crowd. A younger woman took Maggie in another direction. She looked back at her sister with tears in her eyes, pointing to her heart and folding her hands as if in prayer. She wondered when they would ever see each other again.

Months passed and the cold winter temperatures changed into a warming spring. The icy winds were no longer blowing and all the snow had melted. Around the entrance to the village, a meandering stream flowed quietly over odd sized rocks, and down into the valley which now had been covered with different shades of green foliage and many types of colorful wildflowers. Newly sprouted grass vibrated in the gentle breeze. Curling wisps of smoke seemed to float above each tent before drifting away.

Maggie used the hand signals she had learned from her new mother to ask, for at least the hundredth time, when she would be able to see her sister. While waiting for what she knew to be the same answer, she thought, *this isn't so bad. I have been treated decently. I even learned to cook rabbit stew and use pemmican and choke cherries in the buffalo meat we cut into cakes after the meat dried.*

Some days I even sewed some my own clothes. Not able to understand why she couldn't see her sister, Maggie had been rocked to sleep many nights as she cried herself to sleep. Singing Dove was a different kind of mother, who worked everyday to help her adjust.

One morning after their chores were completed, Singing Dove took Maggie's hand and motioned for her to follow as she walked outside their tent. Elizabeth stood there, alone, looking tired and nervous.

"I can't believe you are finally here, Elizabeth; I've been so worried all these months. How are you doing? Do you like your new family? Are they nice to you?" Her words tumbled out slowly; she had not spoken English since her arrival, many months ago. She ran to her older sister and gave her a hug.

"So many questions, Maggie, wait a minute. I am only here for one reason, to get your help sewing beads on a wedding dress. The chief's daughter is getting married soon. I told them you used to sew at home all the time, hoping they might let you help. Now we'll get to see each other everyday." Her words came out very slowly too.

"This is such good news, Elizabeth. I'm so glad to get to see you every day." She felt so happy for the first time in months.

As the weeks passed, beadwork sewing became tedious and tiresome. Maggie felt thrilled to see her sister everyday but unhappy to hear Elizabeth's version of her life there as she said, "I've thought of nothing but ways to escape!"

"But Elizabeth, their ways aren't so bad. I sure do miss some of Ma's cooking and the games we used to play and, believe it or not,

92

even going to school. This is just another life, one we aren't used to yet." Her eyebrows scrunched up in concern for her sister's thoughts.

"Don't say YET, 'cause this sounds as though you want to stay." She felt shock and surprise at her younger sister's ideas. Her brown eyebrows rose on a wrinkled forehead.

"Elizabeth, where would we go?"

One night after dinner, Maggie heard war chants and singing. She felt an old fear returning. Standing outside her tent she saw many warriors dancing around a blazing fire. Her legs started shaking. Was it only a year ago many of these same warriors were circling their wagon train at a fast pace? Even though she felt afraid and scared now, she remembered how surprised she was to see horses moving without needing any control as their riders sat still and straight shooting arrows from their bows and never slowing down in any way. She even remembered how one man took care to wipe the blood off her sister's leg as he carefully pulled out an arrow and covered the wound with some type of salve and a piece of cloth. While looking at the smoke from this campfire, she recalled the smell of smoke from the burning canvas of their wagon.

Singing Dove brought her back into reality as she told her soldiers had been seen in the area and a war party would be going out in the morning. She motioned with hand movements the possibility of them having to leave quickly.

Just before she went to sleep, Maggie remembered the thoughts Elizabeth had shared and she wondered: *could we be rescued and saved from living here?* For a moment she wondered if they could have another life.

Would there be a possibility of going to a nearby fort and live with another family since there was no one left to take them in back in St. Louis? Would she really want to leave Singing Dove and go back to a life with real clothes, no deerskin and no moccasins?

The next morning Maggie watched with awe as the warriors rode proudly in single file out of the village waving their spears. Inside the tent she tried to concentrate on her sewing, wondering if Elizabeth would come over today to help her finish the final row of beads. She questioned herself, wondering if the wedding would even take place.

Loud yelling, continuous shouts and pounding hoofs suddenly caught her attention. As she rushed outside she saw soldiers riding through the other end of the village shooting wildly. Singing Dove yelled for her to come quickly, pointing to the safety of the nearby forest. Maggie felt confused, her mind overwhelmed with choices. She looked at Singing Dove, signing and talking as quickly as possible. Her sister needed to be found first.

While some soldiers rode closer to her area of the village, she saw many of the tents burning. Stinging smoke and dense dust from the horses blocked her view and she wasn't sure which way to run.

"Elizabeth," she screamed as loudly as she could. She became disoriented and wondered which way she should go, stopping in her confusion.

Two soldiers galloped into Maggie's view and she watched their horses move more slowly as they came near her tent. Her freckled arms waved rapidly in the air to catch their attention.

"Over here, over here," she yelled as loudly as she could.

Suddenly they were in front of her, shaking their heads in disbelief. "Little girl, are you alright? Here take my hand and get up on my horse. Are there others?" He offered a strong arm and quickly pulled her up onto the back of his sweating brown horse.

"Yes, my sister." Sweat dripped off his brow and he showed her a small smile; she felt safe for the monent.

As she settled onto the back of the soldier's horse, she noticed his fast breathing. Her troubled eyes searched through the many evergreen trees for Singing Dove, tears falling down her flushed cheeks. *I hope she is safe.*

Suddenly, Elizabeth came staggering out of the thick smoke. Tears streamed down her face as she stumbled over the ground. Maggie called out to her as loudly as possible, "Elizabeth, over here!"

Together they would start another life.

V. WHY NOT ME?

"This is the biggest slumber party ever; why can't I go?" My dark blue eyes darted back and forth from my mother's solemn face to my dad's stern expressionless one. I focused hard to keep tears from forming .

"Dad, just tell me one good reason why I can't go. I haven't been invited to any town parties and I finally get an invitation . . . all the neatest girls from school will be there. I'm the only one from the base who's been asked and I really want to go. You won't even have to drive me since Jody said I could ride home with her after school on Friday. I have no babysitting jobs lined up this week-end and," . . . the non-stop rambling ceased as her dad held up his tanned right hand.

"Stop whining, Emma. You sound like your younger brother instead of someone about to finish high school. There is only one reason you can't go, because I said so. Besides, your mother and I are going out to the Officer's Club next Friday night and you need to babysit your brothers and sister."

"Why can't you ever hire someone else? I'm seventeen years old and I NEVER get to do anything I want. I always have to stay here and watch them. This is sooo unfair."

"Just once, Mom, please?" I started to loose control and didn't want to make a scene by crying.

"Don't bring your mother into this; my decision is final."

Uncontrolled tears now flowed from my eyes as I rushed out of the living room and down the hall. My bedroom door slammed a little too hard and an immediate response was heard as a loud voice thundered into the back of the house.

"Young lady, come back here this minute."

"Dear, can't you give her a few minutes to calm down? You can see she is quite upset." Marie Landrum, the ever calming source in the family looked at her husband with care and concern.

"Don't you think you were a little too hard on her? We could let David sit since we are only going over to the club and it is only a mile away. Cindy and Jon aren't babies anymore. I think he could certainly handle them for a few hours. Won't you re-consider?"

A few minutes later, a knock on my bedroom door took my attention away from having to turn down my music. My mom turned the handle on the solid pine bedroom door and entered slowly.

"Mom, why can't you stand up for me, just once? I never ask to do something special, and now I have a chance to do something really fun." I dabbed my eyes with a tissue.

"Emma, you are our first child, and I know how difficult this is for you. Your dad is realizing you are growing up. He's having a little trouble with you almost finishing high school. After four short years in college, you'll be gone forever. I know going to a slumber party won't hurt you."

She sighed and continued, "It's just our lack of planning because we have always counted on you to be here. After you finish college you'll be having your own family one day. I can only hope you'll understand when you become a parent."

"At the rate I'm going, Mom, I'll never get married because I can't go outside this house to meet someone. I still can't believe dad is allowing me to go away to college." I looked outside one of the large bedroom windows to a bright sunny day, with not a cloud in sight.

"Besides, I 'm not sure if getting married and having children is for me," I sighed. "Didn't you ever . . . ? Never mind, I'm just not up for one of your deprived childhood stories now."

"Now dear, you aren't playing fair. The only reason I tell you about my childhood is so you'll realize how lucky you are to have a father who loves and provides for you."

"Mom, please. I just don't want to hear this again. I'm really sorry your father died when you were so young, but Dad is so mean to us. Do you think I'm being unreasonable? Do I go out every week-end like the other kids? No, I'm babysitting for someone else so I don't have to sit here." I pushed my dark brown bangs off my forehead and fell back onto my bed, sobbing.

"Give me a little time dear. I'll talk to your dad again. I'm going to suggest David sit for your brother and sister this time. We won't be out late anyway since we're just going over to the club. You are right, you don't have much of a social life and your senior year in high school should be more memorable. You are a good girl, Emma, and I really am so glad you've been able to babysit for us regularly. You do well in school and I know you'll make something of yourself. Please, just be patient."

"Mom, you always say the same thing. It's time he realized I'm not a little girl anymore. I should fight my own battles now, not you for me." I leaned a pillow against the soft yellow wall as I continued to plead my case. "Is there any valid reason for me not to go to this party?"

"Why don't you come in, set the table and help me get dinner ready? We'll see how the evening goes. We can talk more about this after the dishes are washed."

Dinner dragged on as the plates were passed down to their mom, who filled each one with a piece of fried chicken, mashed potatoes and green beans with onions and bacon pieces. Once again my dad became Major Landrum, who controlled the conversation by asking all four of us a question about current events. This had been going on for years, and I couldn't wait to leave home and not be quizzed on potential problems in the world or another geography lesson. None of my friends ever had this type conversation. I always felt glad when he had to fly and be gone for dinner.

Even though David and Cindy were supposed to clean up after dinner, I told them they could owe me. I took the dirty dishes into the kitchen and filled the sink with hot soapy water. After I put on yellow rubber gloves, I looked out the window toward the inlet of salt water and realized I would miss living on an Air Force base with everything we needed so close. And most of all, I'd miss the beach and sound of the waves crashing to shore.

I sure hope we get to stay here four years, so I won't have to go to a new home from college.

"Mom, when I finish the dishes can I walk over to Peggy's? Her brother Zach is home from Florida State University and she wants to take him over to the teen club tonight. We won't be out late either, I promise."

"All right dear. When you are finished in the kitchen, you can leave. I'll talk to your dad again. Have fun and be sure to say hello to Peggy's parents."

After she left, fourteen year old David and twelve year old Cindy sat down on the couch where their dad read the evening paper.

"Dad, I'm a teenager now and have been helping Jon since he was born. I can do this. You won't be far away and if something does happen, I know you can be home in less then ten minutes." He spoke with determination, glad for a chance to be in charge if he would be allowed to babysit.

Cindy twisted a strand of white blond hair around her finger as she gathered up some courage to support her older brother and sister.

"Daddy, we can too stay by ourselves. David is only three years younger than Emma, and I helped change Jon's diapers and watched him many times. Now he is five. We can take good care of him." She smiled a genuine show of support for this idea.

"Yeah, she's right Dad. Jon will go to bed early and we can just play a board game or read. We won't even answer the phone or the door. Can I just have one try?"

Mrs. Landrum stood in the kitchen doorway, listening to her younger children voice their opinion, something rarely allowed. *They are growing up too.*

"Children you have brought up some good ideas. Let me speak to your dad for a little while and see if his mind can be changed." They turned to leave, knowing they had indeed been fortunate to be allowed to speak this much. In David and Jon's room, Cindy took out the monopoly game. Jon sat at a small table to color.

After another thirty minute discussion, Mrs. Landrum saw a small smile creep onto her husband's mouth. "So you think they can handle themselves do you?"

He put his arm around his wife of eighteen years, then looked out the large living room window to watch waves lap up to the shoreline, a calming effect on him. "You are right dear, in one more year she'll be gone to the university. Just because my sister couldn't do these things, doesn't mean she can't. This is a different world." He stopped talking for a minute and then asked another question. "You know these people, right?"

"Yes I do. Jody's mom plays bridge with us. They decided not to live in base housing and are renting a house closer to town. I know this is difficult for you too, but the time has come when our little bird needs to strengthen her wings and fly a little."

"Guess I'm really outnumbered. Alright, I will change my opinion. When she comes home, tell her she can go. I'm going out to the driving range and hit a bucket of golf balls. "

He yelled down the hall before he left. "Okay kids. You won this round. I've changed my mind."

About an hour later, I came in the front door, a frown on my face and wrinkled eyebrows tightly knitted together on a creased forehead, still feeling overwhelmed with disappointment. I walked over to the couch where mom read the base newspaper and plopped down next to her.

"I have some good news for you. Your sister and brother really put in a few good words for you, and your dad agreed David will babysit. I think I'm seeing the beginning of a new dad." She looked into her oldest daughter's unhappy face, just starting to form a smile, and patted her shoulder.

"Why don't you call Jody right now? Tell her you can come to the slumber party."

Writers spend many long hours with their new friends, the characters they create. Sometimes they need an extra pair of eyes to read with a new perspective.

Thanks so much to my family, Harvey, Carole Anne and Jon who helped me remember some of our experiences from so long ago when we traveled to France.

Thanks also to my sons Jason (cover design) Richard (editing) and to my friends Becky and Lynda for continuing to proofread again and again. Any errors missed are on me.

Please don't hesitate to contact me at the email address at the beginning to the book to give me your ideas on these stories.

Merci. Thanks so much. ENJOY.

Made in the USA
Monee, IL
07 July 2026

56552670R00059